The Earth Priest

A Factional Mythography

(Illustrated)

Alan Richardson

with

V. M. Firth

I don't have a web site, agent or manager, am not on LinkedIn, don't do blogs, vlogs or lectures any more after upsetting the good folk of GlasVegasBury. A more detailed list of my published work can be found somewhere on Amazon Books.

As before, I price this at the minimum suggested by KDP, which means:

a) I get two pence for every copy I sell.
b) people might be tempted to buy one.

If you don't, it means you don't love Dion Fortune.

Anyone with a pressing need to contact me can do so via: *alric@blueyonder.co.uk* but please don't attach your manuscripts and ask for 'an honest opinion', because I don't want to hurt people, and will always fib.

Alan Richardson is the most original writer on magic in the world, and this is certainly his greatest, weirdest and most original book.
Melusine Draco

This is almost a prose poem whose rhythms will have deep effects upon the reader, and propel them on to outward as well as inward adventures once its open Secret is revealed.
Judy Hall

The Earth Priest is an initiatory novel that weaves fact and fiction in a way that no-one ever has. It is not a 'Sea Priestess' parody, but a powerful stand-alone book with as many geo-spiritual levels as the character of the Earth Priest himself.
Margaret Haffenden

'Wilfred Maxwell's private diaries were heavily redacted by his ghost-writer 'Dion Fortune'. When these were finally published as 'The Sea Priestess' and marketed as fiction, the book concealed more than it ever revealed about what *really* happened in that remote Fort in Somersetshire between the Wars. In fact, the heroin addict Maxwell had a lot to hide, and his amanuensis went to very clever lengths to protect him.

'Here in 'The Earth Priest' is a different insight about the events in that remote and haunted place, as told by another participant. And one who reveals a secret that was hiding in plain sight then - and even more so today, a century later…'

This is a heavily-illustrated, footnoted, 'Factional Mythography'. Although 'The Earth Priest' was started on a light-hearted whim, it seemed almost immediately that 'V.M. Firth' wanted her own (often teasing) input, and so the book turned into something very odd and not at all what I originally planned. I like to believe that she enjoyed every moment. Purists of DNF might want to brace themselves for what follows...

The present book is necessarily dedicated to…

Violet M. Firth
Violet M. Evans
Dion Fortune
D.N.F.
V.M. Steele
Vi
Fluff
Rhea

…in the hope that
They
will accept the thieving literary ways
of
my
Inner Magpie.

And as ever and always, for millions and millions of years…

Margaret

Some **published books**

Geordie's War – foreword by Sting
Aleister Crowley and Dion Fortune
The Inner Guide to Egypt *with Billie John*
Priestess - the Life and Magic of Dion Fortune
Magical Gateways
The Magical Kabbalah
The Google Tantra - How I became the first Geordie to raise the Kundalini.
new edition Sex and Light – How to Google your way to God Hood.
The Old Sod *with* Marcus Claridge
Working with Inner Light *with Jo Clark*
Earth God Risen
Gate of Moon
Dancers to the Gods
Inner Celtia *with David Annwn*
Letters of Light
Me, mySelf and Dion Fortune
Bad Love Days
Short Circuits
The Templar Door
Searching for Sulis
The Quantum Simpleton
The Sea Priest
Dark Magery
Al-Khemy
Visions at Ewyas
Visions of Paviland
Neurolithica – foreword by Uri Geller
Kim's Book
The Inner Realms of Christine Hartley
Scattering Light – with (somehow) William G. Gray
Elphame

<u>Fiction</u>
The Giftie
On Winsley Hill
The Fat Git – the Story of a Merlin
The Great Witch Mum – *illustrated by Caroline Jarosz*
Dark Light – a neo-Templar Time Storm
The Movie Star
Shimmying Hips

du Lac
The Lightbearer
Twisted Light
The Moonchild
The Giftie – in her own words.
Old Light
Boudicca – scripted with Mark Colmar

As Yet Unpublished and un-filmed Scripts – free to a good home…
(We had some fun trying to get these produced, meeting directors, actors, producers, financiers and many others in this field. In the event, despite huge promises, all disappeared at the last moment like faery gold.)

On Winsley Hill
The Enchanter (from the novella The Fat Git)
The Giftie

Introduction, Explanation
and...
Slightly Shame-faced Apology.

I will tell anyone and everyone, jabbing my finger in the air at them if challenged, that *The Sea Priestess* is one of the most beautiful books ever written. I will have no arguments about this. No-one – and I mean no-one, whether you're a Baby Boomer, Millennial, Generation Z or someone born beyond Time and Space on another planet entirely – can match 'Dion Fortune' for the hypnotic and infallible rhythms of her prose, the power of imagery, plus the clarity, purity and sheer evocative power of almost every sentence.

I was a teenager when I stumbled upon a copy of *The Sea Priestess* in the library at Ashington, in Northumberland. I can still see its place on the shelf, next to another that was called *Moon Magic*. It was two-thirds of the way up on the western wall overlooking the Town Hall. Although I was scrawny-tall, I had to reach up slightly to get them. Somehow the books called to me, and so I've been a firm champion of Libraries and a believer in the extraordinary power of the Library Angel ever since.

I was already obsessed by 'The Occult' – dreadful, ugly word, that - and felt that these particular tomes by the crassly-named author (whom I assumed was American) might contain a few nuggets of wisdom and help me with my own cosmically-important Quest. It was my belief even then, that if an otherwise rubbish book gave me just *one* valuable sentence, then its whole existence and cost of purchase was justified. And so I borrowed both books and went home with a certain curiosity about what I might find.

In the event I was Whelmed (is there still such a word?) and even perhaps Initiated by the rhythms and energies that flowed out of every page and into my very soul. I was never quite the same boy again.

But you wouldn't have liked me then. Few did. Looking back on myself, even I tend to squirm. Like most teenagers I was, in my own mind, Omniscient; though no doubt in the minds of others around me I was simply Omni-noxious, if there is such a word[1]. I was going through puberty, virgin, troubled, arrogant-without-substance, battered and

---
[1] An inner voice (it must be mine!) is saying that I'm still the same!

perhaps damaged on emotional levels by my fraught upbringing. But after a few hours reading I knew that *The Sea Priestess* was the most awesome book in the whole history of the world - even better than *Shane* - and was about to heal scars in my soul that I didn't know I had. While my Mam and Dad were killing each other on triple levels downstairs (physical, emotional, verbal) I absorbed this book in a sitting, feeling that it was singing to me, seeing the locales writ large, never imagining that they actually existed and that one day I would be prompted to explore them in person.

To me, despite my ignorance of the world beyond the coal-mining town of Ashington, this writer with the crass pen-name of 'Dion Fortune' showed me another realm that reeked with ancient, otherworldly wisdoms and the magical possibilities of Males and Females. Yet while she offered me revelatory teachings about sexuality that must have been explosive in those sex-repressed decades before the Second World War, I think that readers today have pretty much reached her level of Gnosis about those polarities. Today, almost a century after the book was conceived and then published, the teachings that Dion Fortune expressed via the character of 'Vivien le Fay Morgan' can now seem tame and perhaps even risible.

Just don't sneer in my presence, that's all I need say.

Yet this is not meant as a pastiche, or a 'Sea Priestess' parody. I can only confess that 'V.M. Firth' seemed to hover over me at times and nudge me into writing it. Certainly, it was never my intention to try and match or mirror the prose. No-one could do that. Perhaps, at first, I *was* intending to rip-off the story line and have some light-hearted, recuperative fun with a gentle parody. Yet as soon as I started scribbling in the Atrium of Trowbridge Library, the 'Tone' came in quickly and the book took shape with 'VMF' as an interested and often amused participant. The best I can describe this notion of 'Tone' is that it suffuses my psyche, an inner song, a thrumming. Things happen, images arise, startling connections that are relevant to my own inner life are prompted. I don't go into any sort of trance; you could sit on the next table and see me as no more than absorbed in the writing or reading. In comparison, the 'Tone' of *The Sea Priestess* and the later *Moon Magic* is to me like a great symphony in the Royal Albert Hall. My own 'Tone' for *The Earth Priest* is no more than something you might hear from some jolly buskers in Bath Abbey Courtyard, easily lost on the breeze.

Then again, looking back, I'm reminded of a throwaway comment made to me some 40 years ago that was possibly responsible for all of this.

I was staying with Dolores Ashcroft-Nowicki and her husband Michael in Jersey, and was curious about the latter's own 'Places of Power'. This notion of Earth Consciousness and Spirits of Place had always obsessed me. I would never ask people, as long-haired pseudo-Hippies like myself used to do, what their Star Sign was, but always what Places they came from; what ancient Sites might have touched or inspired them. I assumed that Michael (a genuine Adept 'if ever there was one') would reel off: Glastonbury Tor, Stonehenge, Avebury, Silbury, West Kennet (all of which he knew well) or even places in his native Poland. Not a bit of it. Instead he replied instantly:

'Brent Knoll'.

'Eh?'

'Brent. Knoll. Brent Knoll. There is *real* power at that place.'

'I've never heard of it! Where exactly is it?'

He told me.

I had no certain idea where this was, but remembered that *The Sea Priestess* was set in very real but slightly disguised places, although this was not commonly known at the time. Wherever you live in the world, when reading this, you can now explore these yourself by the 'Remote Viewing' made possible by *Google Earth*. Peer down upon the Fort at the tip of Brean Down, that is described in *The Sea Priestess* as 'Bell Head'. Then scroll across a very few miles to Brent Knoll, that was given the name of 'Bell Knowle'. These are very solid places. I suppose she had to disguise Brent Knoll in particular, lest the villagers be upset by descriptions of human sacrifice and Atlantean Sex Magick that she said underlay their modest, quiet hill in primordial times before the priests came.

For some reason I became increasingly intrigued by Dion's descriptions of 'Bell Knowle' that still floated around in my shallow tidal memory. And I kept hearing Mike's insistent words: 'There is *real* power at that place'.

When I re-read *The Sea Priestess* for the first time in decades I was struck by things I'd never noticed before, that I think 'VMF' wanted me to point out now. I realised what a useless little shit the narrator 'Wilfred Maxwell' was. If readers care to defragment their own memories by re-reading it as I did, they will – I promise – see all sorts of things that were hidden beneath the flowing tides of her prose. In my hazy fondness for the book I remembered him as an exemplar of the essentially useless Modern Man in that era (the 1930s), who desperately needed some archetypal Goddess Power to get him sorted. Yet in sentence after sentence, image after image, I see that she was describing (quite subtly) someone who was alcoholic, a drug addict, a sneering, snobbish, cross-dressing, sister-beating mummy's boy and closet gay, who wrestled with his hidden sexuality as men *had* to do in that dreadful era.

While I found that intriguing, not to say eye-opening, I was more taken by my notion that her descriptions of the Caves Within the Hill got somewhat side-tracked. A generation of readers such as myself were once slightly obsessed by the Sea Priestess's 'secret and sacred cave' we fancied was lost within Brean Down. But the *important* one, where all the inner action took place, was clearly the textually swept-aside Bell Knowle.

On reflection, I probably *did* start writing *The Earth Priest* out of light-hearted whimsey. I needed something to do, to help me recuperate after a heart attack, to reassure myself that 'It' hadn't all gone away. However, it quickly became apparent that the writing invoked on a daily basis the 'Tone' I mentioned, and a sense of VMF's presence with the usual 'Signs Following' that have always seemed to me 'meaninglessly meaningful'. This would make a small story in itself and one in which the Spirit of Place that lurks around Brent Knoll has manifested all sorts of striking events and quite startling synchronicities. I still haven't been there in person, and perhaps never will. There are all sorts of unusual things you can Google about the hill and its inherent Beings and histories if you care to, particularly with respect to Sir Edern *aka* Sir Ider. Let me know what you find.

Yet even the concepts of Tone, Presence and Identity don't really explain the process. I suppose 'Daniel Steele' is my equivalent of the Priest of the Moon – something artificially created that achieves its own (temporary) existence that only *I* can feel. I'm rather hoping that you might sense it yourself, in the prose rhythms which follow.

I know full well that I will get sneering comments from the die-hard fans of 'Vivien le Fay Morgan' and her creatrix Dion Fortune for writing this but I'm too old to worry about that. After a lifetime crafting my own kind of magic(k), often with no obvious or immediate results, I have learned just to let go and see what, if anything, might rise to the surface.

Most readers visualise the remote, isolated Fort of the Sea Priestess as facing out into the wild Atlantic. I've added some pictures and maps to clarify geographies and perhaps help them pick up their own 'Spirits of Inner Place' as they read…

The world of the Sea Priestess

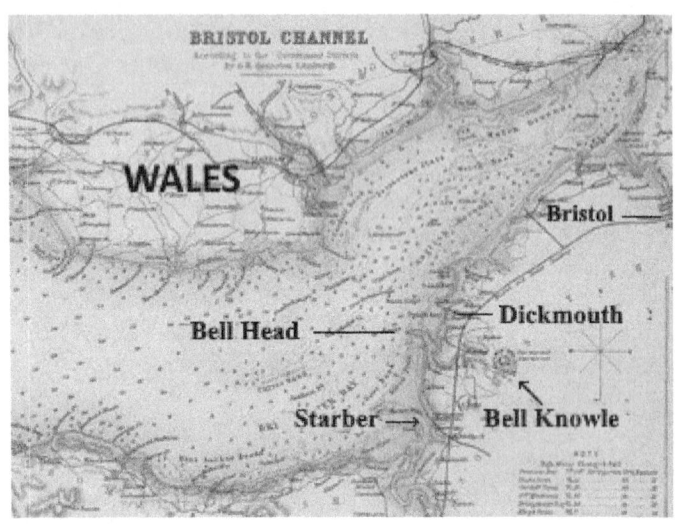

The world of the Earth Priest

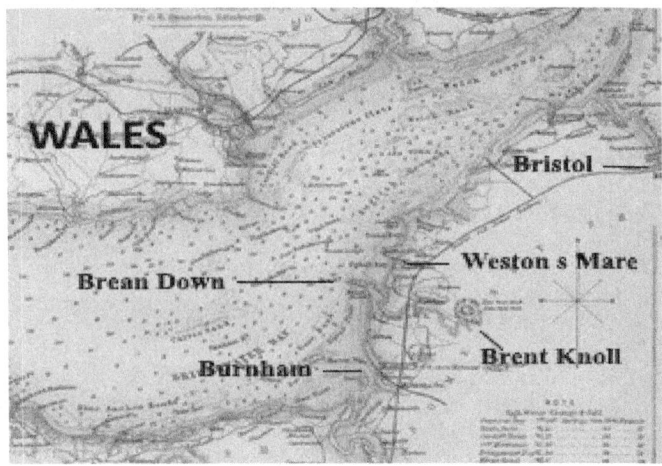

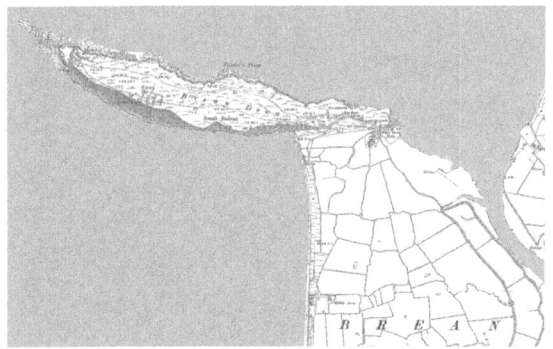

The long shaft of 'Bell Head' *aka* Brean Down

Brean Down Fort

Wilfred Maxwell's drug-induced drawing of 'Bell Head'

Courtesy of the Somerset HER – (Historic Environment Record)

The curiously heart-shaped Brent Knoll *aka* 'Bell Knowle', where Daniel Steele and Vivien le Fay Morgan felt the *real* stuff began.

Edern ap Nudd

The Earth Priest.

*I will have to **kill** her.*

I find myself saying this out loud as tides of anger rise and threaten to drown me.

Who? I have had people respond, usually fearfully when they take one look at my rough ruggedness, but I can never explain. Not easily. She has wrapped and lapped herself around my own hard life, flowing and splashing over everything I am, leaving little silver bubbles that pop into teasing whispers of scorn

*I **will** have to kill her*, even though she seems to be indissoluble, with cold and unimaginable depths that none can ever explore lest the pressure of her darkness crushes them.

*I will **have** to kill her*, else she will wear me down as she always does, does with everyone, until I am nothing more than a thin spindle of thought that leaves all my remaining substance displayed in worn strata of shame.

I *will have to kill her.*

Me. Myself. Who else dare try? If I do not, she will envelope everything, everyone, destroying but ever-withdrawing, leaving only bubbles that sigh into nothingness.

Who? You might dare ask when you know that I am not a lunatic but solid as rock, and that you will always be safe with me. And then I can only answer:

What, *is the word. You might ask* **What** *is she?*

So... 'What' is she?

She is a Sea Priestess.

I should explain, though it may take me geological time-spans to get near the truth.

I first saw her on the 22nd of February 1922. A date that can sit easily on the strata of anyone's memory. Wednesday. I was in the war-wearied little town of Weston-super-Mare in Somersetshire, where billboards for *The Times* proclaimed headlines of Egypt being granted Independence. I doubt if the good folk of the town were over-excited by this; they were more intrigued by this Marconi chap the previous week broadcasting new things into the aethers, for whatever purpose few could fathom, and also the vicious and as yet unsolved murder in the nearby salt-marshes.

I had just strolled along the Royal Parade until it merged into Marine Parade lined with monstrous old Victorian houses that edged the street like a row of off-white, broken molars. When the tide came in along with a westerly wind bringing the smell of sea-weed and salt air, this 'posh' part of the town squealed. Try it yourself… put the tip of your tongue along the bottom of your upper teeth and suck. That's the sound you would hear from this street. Maybe part of it was the wind in the gaps of decaying buildings caused by the collapse of the housing market which had financially crippled more than a few of the worthies. Or maybe it was simply dead souls screeching about the catastrophic loss of their sons from the Great War and the grandchildren who would now never grow up in them and learn how to manage the servant class.

The day was dull with scudding, massing clouds and needle-sharp bursts of rain. I wanted nothing more than to get home before the storm, yet I had to make a quick visit to 'Maxwell and Partner' Estate Agents to pick up my very young daughter Fleur, who was being looked after in the back rooms by a sort of baby-sitter. I was surprised to see that spindly fool Wilfred Maxwell himself there, almost dancing on the spot as his customer – a tall, elegant woman whose back was toward me – signed a hefty document spread on the old mahogany desk that was covered with ink stains and rune-like gouges that really needed sanded down.

He was probably telling her about the 'sea view' that her new property – wherever it was – would have. That in itself was wicked, and caught out many strangers with more money than sense who had bought up properties along the Front without ever waiting for the waves to go out. If so, they would find that there was no 'sea', but the tidal River Severn that flowed up to the long stretch of golden sand and created the illusion.

With the tide out, there was a whole mile of pure alluvial mud before you could reach any water. Mud and hidden quicksands that had claimed many a holiday-maker with their Kiss Me Quick hats and their toy bucket and spades. Particularly toward Brean. Weston-super-*Mud* is what the locals called it.

Yet Brean Down itself was ancient and pure, on all sorts of levels. Learned men who adored Darwin had found within the Sand Cliff on its south side fragments of reindeer, aurochs, bison, wolves and mammoths. I have these within my own strata.

We all do.

Had this woman fallen for his spiel?

Well, he seems to have fallen for *her*.

This is Miss Morgan, he said, eyes shining, and it was either because the contract had just saved his failing business of White Elephantine properties or because the woman had bewitched him.

I can see why.

She was tall and slight, and wore a black velvet Tam O'Shanter on her head and a black fur coat with enormous collar and cuffs. The Tam was pulled down over her ear and the huge collar was up, concealing her face from this angle. She stiffened for a moment and paused from whatever it was she was signing. I had the odd notion that she sensed me, or maybe had just sniffed the damp mud on my work boots and the tang of my Craven pipe tobacco in the top pocket of my working coat that contrasted with her own surprising whiff of... musk, I should say. She finished her signature with a flourish and turned away from Maxwell but toward me. I saw that her eyes were an eerie, unnatural green and almost almond shaped lids; her thin but heavily-painted lips of pillar-box scarlet gave the slightest stretch and rise to one side as if at some joke.

Hello I heard in my head. Or did *I* say that silently?

I knew her. She knew me. Old knowledge whispering from a time before Time. There was a pure and silken flow in the actual room, like living air. Stillness that is sentient, embracing. The world had stopped turning. No past, no future. No love, though. We were both beyond that.

Yet Wilfred Maxwell was oblivious to this and like a little puppy. I don't know what breed as I've never liked dogs: something small and pitiful that yaps a lot. He was excited. Nervous. Eager to please or impress. Legs twitching as he almost danced on the spot, red-faced with fever. Then the promised storm burst upon us and rain punched against the windows and Miss Morgan raised one thin crescent moon of an eyebrow toward me as if to say:

See?

Like a liquid Hades, Maxwell joked in his thin voice, though no-one smiled at his posh-school sally.

Very dimpsey, I countered, using the common deep Zummerzet that you rarely hear now except among the grey-beards and ancients.

Dimpsey? she asked, intrigued or amused. *Is that from the Enochian?*

From Somerset.

I like the sound of it! And the meaning?

Dimpsey. Like the rain and light now. It means the half-light which comes at the end of a long day. Like now.

Maxwell frowned and glared at me. I had said just one earthy word but he feared that I had already spoiled his chances of finding the sublime and impossible love he so clearly craved.

I must say now that I never had much Time for him. He was 35 and still a virgin. An old Army Sergeant like me can tell these things. Not that there was anything wrong with that, but every young man I ever met in the War wanted to lose their virginity before they died (though mine, as a married man in *this* phase of my existence, had long since gone). No-one in Weston knew how he had avoided being called up. Apparently, he had been given White Feathers in the street by young women trying to shame him into Doing His Duty, but I was a too busy in Flanders to know if that was true.

I had heard from his business partner Scottie (of whom more later), that he suffered very badly both from asthma and even more from his powerful mother. *Apparently* he spent his time in his bedroom devoted to reading books on Theosophy and Christian Science and writing letters to various worthies. I was told this by his spinster sister, Ethel, who had organised a group known as the 'Friendly Girls'. This amicable coven met in the basement of their mother's huge house. Wilfred and Ethel had nothing in common and sometimes hated each other. *Apparently* that sort of thing is usual but as a perpetual orphan myself, I wouldn't know.

Now Ethel, who did more for the poor of the community than Wilfred ever would, told me that some girls had tried to be a little more than just 'friendly' and were often rudely rebuffed. Well, there were so few men left in those years that even a weed like him was worth a try. In the event, they ended up rolling their eyes while uttering those words 'Confirmed Bachelor' that had both protected and condemned a certain type of male in those years.

I didn't care if he was homosexual. They were a hidden and secretive race in the 1920s, avoiding the light, coming out when they dared and with *whom* they dared - that is to say Believers - trusting few, fearful of strangers. No wonder that they were often nicknamed 'Fairies', after that marvellous Lost Race which inhabited the Earth before Humans were even imagined. They adopted similar stratagems in order to survive: shape-shifting, hiding in dark and secret places where they could come out and dance to the stars.

I doubt if he even knew himself what he was, he was so curiously 'wet', as they used to say. Yet here he was with 'Miss Morgan' – a pseudonym if ever there was one - his face like a lighted fart, aroused, somehow, by her very presence. I have known 'glamour boys' seemingly able to function with older, motherly types, so perhaps this explained his puppy-like excitement. Or am I being a bit new-fangled and Psychological here?

It amused me, later, to hear this 'Sea Priestess' boasting about a kingdom that was neither material nor spiritual but a strange kingdom of its own. Those were her words, as recorded by The Drip, as I thought of him. And she also added, because she always let her words pour out in a continuous stream, that there were 'two worships, one of the sun and one of the moon'.

Well, so there was, but there were actually *four:* of the sun, moon, earth and stars.

I need not boast, as she always did when she found a soft man with muddy soul, but the worship of the Earth Kingdom is material *and* spiritual.

And by Kingdom I don't mean those puny clusters that call themselves 'countries', with their politics and governments and leaders and customs and wars. I mean that which is underfoot. Always and forever. Infinite. Everlasting, Earths without end.

Find it yourself now. Put your foot down, flat. Press hard. It doesn't matter where you are, or when, or what you wear on your feet or what is underneath them. Feel the Earth in its entirety, pressing back upward, pressing upward through your legs and spine and neck and cranium. Listen, listen, listen…Try not to fidget. Peace, be still. Still, find peace. This upward pressure is the Earth's applause, its roaring praise, its silent hallelujah to its own glory and eternal power.

And what do you need to be an Earth Priest or Priestess? Rituals? Chants? Incense? Drugs? Robed circlings one way and then the other? Sacrifices – human or otherwise?

No need. Just be human. Simple. Each earth-step is its own kind of prayer. Walk. Empty your mind. Be a camera. Walk each step as a silent invocation. Feel your own kingdom underfoot and send your mind down through the granite and basalt crust, pierce the searing lava flows and break through mantle and lithosphere and plunge your thoughts down to the innermost sun of the burning, ever-exploding core.

Listen, listen listen… because one day, as you continue to live a simple and unobtrusive life, you will hear the greeting from the deepest and most buried stars that whisper….

Hello!

So there we were on February 22 1922, facing each other within the dimpsey - the half-light at the end of a long day in Somerset. I had just spent the previous few days repairing and reshaping the old dry-stone walls that surrounded old Mr Chichester's cottage along the bay at Kewstoke. It took me some time because he insisted I use stones from the remains of short-lived 4th Century hermitage that had itself replaced a small church atop of Brean Down. The journey back and forth was hard for me, but old Chichester deemed it worthwhile and paid me accordingly.

Maxwell, on that day, looked like a non-swimmer trying to rise to the surface of a deep pool, almost snorting as he fought for air and sought for words to help him float. He could have killed me then, if mental power could do so such a thing as his mother's Christian Scientists apparently believed. It was Miss Morgan who pulled him up and out.

Mr. Maxwell, it is all agreed then. As part of our agreement I will need some considerable work done on the house. At the moment it is a shell. I will need a craftsman to get started before I pay the first instalment, someone who is on the level.

The vendor's face lightened.

Then have this fellow here! My partner Scottie contracts him for repairs and maintenance of all our properties, including extensions and new builds. What d'ye say old chap?

Old chap. That's how he described me in his book: '*Old* Bindling' he called me, as if I were a dodderer. He was probably afraid to use my real name in case I sued, even though I had long since disappeared from his soggy life. Then again, he seemed afraid of everything and no-one could have said it was due to shell-shock.

'Old Chap' smiled Miss Morgan, looking hard at me, her scorn and other things splashing around. She cast a curious eye over my clothes:

Citrine, olive, russet and black she mused with a sort of 'tut tut tut' at the faded colours of my fustian shirt, khaki trousers, old army boots and older trench-coat that still had marks on the shoulders made by the straps of the haversack. A sharp contrast indeed to her almost iridescent displays of blue, turquoise, and sea green.

She stretched out one manicured finger with a painted nail and flicked at the wearied, silver regimental badge that I kept pinned on my like a medal.

What is that device, 'old chap'?

A cannon.

The wind outside shrieked like a banshee and scraped against the windows. Water and Air and ancient Death. That was always the tone of 'Miss Morgan'.

I like the motto: Ubuque.

Everywhere.

You are Artillery. You are a destroyer of worlds. But can you build a whole new world for me here.

Where is 'here'?

Maxwell was swirling around. He had to stop this:

Miss Morgan has bought the old fort at the very tip of Brean Down. It needs a lot of work.

I'd have said more and questioned whether the sale of government property like this was actually legal, but then the door to the back room burst open and the truest joy burst in.

Daddy! cried my tiny daughter Fleur, clutching the paintings she had been doing with Ethel.

I cannot tell you how much my heart still leaps when I remember that Word, the first she had ever said from the darkness of her beginning and mine, that continuous joy from Fleur's lips, the warmth of her cuddles and excitement at the daft pictures of whales and octopii and sea snakes that she waved like flags.

Wilfred Maxwell rolled his eyes toward Miss Morgan.

Miss Morgan frowned at me: an ancient sort of movement of her face that left two curious lines stretching upward between her brows.

But the girl is a... a Mongol!

What did she mean by 'But'? How *dare* she take that tone. How *dare* Maxwell sneer. I could break his slippery spine (if he had one) with a single punch. Fleur had more goodness, grace, kindness, understanding and love within her tiny self than his whole generation could ever muster. She gave me what many people never know, no matter how long they live: unconditional love.[2]

Then the door creaked again and Ethel Maxwell emerged, brushing back her hair, handing me Fleur's coat for the walk home, plus more of the things she had been making for me.

She is such a sweetie, Mr. Steele. You are a lucky man.

Thank you, Miss Maxwell, I am indeed.

Together we helped Fleur into her little red wellingtons and our brows bashed for a moment and we smiled.

Start tomorrow 'Mr Steele?', said my new employer, the Great Diluter who saw and knew everything about me and who would reduce strong medicines such as human love into mere drops.

If I'd known what was to happen, I'd have killed her then.

Maxwell's sister had always been kind to me. In fact Ethel Maxwell helped me out with my small daughter after the Spanish Flu took my wife on the very last day of the War[3]. Her own father (long since departed) must have been a bit scholarly to give her that old-fashioned name, which I later learned means 'Noble'. Well, this Ethel was a dowdy, 'sensible' sort of young woman when I first appeared. She may have hoped that I was about to be some sort of gallant knight in her life because I noticed that she smartened herself up when our encounters became regular because of little Fleur.

Ethel had a very slight scoliosis of the spine that she tried to mask by clothes and careful movements and was always more comfortable sitting, when she felt she could hide it. She had often flirted with me in her own, awkward, faux-gentrified way, involving lots of blushing and hesitant speech but soon accepted that I was a rock-solid widower, immovable. I think she felt all the better then. She was kind, though,

---
[2] Steele never lived to hear the ugly medical term 'Mongolism' replaced with that of 'Down Syndrome' in the 1970s.
[3] The 1918-20 pandemic, commonly known within the UK as Spanish Flu, killed a minimum of 25-50 million people worldwide.

and especially good with Fleur, taking her for long walks along the promenade and onto the new Grand Pier and spending wet afternoons such as that one doing things in the back room with scissors and paint, glue and card and trying to impart skills that my great, leathery killing-hands could never master.

Such things as kindness and gentleness are solid considerations in an Age that was anything but.

Of course, you have to take my word for most of this. And no man's words should ever be writ in concrete.

I should in all fairness point out that Wilfred Maxwell wrote his own highly-inaccurate account of this time and had it published privately. He disguised the characters and with schoolboy smut renamed the places as Dickmouth, Dickford and Narrow Dick – with the long erect shaft of Brean Down was called Bell Head. Every soldier in the British Army used 'Bell' as slang for his own tool. Bell Head – honestly! People with no sense of humour always laugh at their own jokes because no-one else will. They never realise this. How can a drip know it's a drip? The curvature of the surrounding liquid deflects straight vision. Eternal Schoolboy that he was, he probably thought these names were hilarious. See him sniggering away at the turn of every page. Scottie, his dour business partner, said he paid a lot of money for a female ghost writer in London to help him out, and it was she who suggested the name *The Sea Priestess* for the title. If you ever want a different take then you should track down 'Scottie', whose real name you would easily find were you to scour *Kelly's Directory - Somersetshire* for 1922. I don't think his story would be too different to mine.

It all began for Maxwell at dusk when, under the influence of dope, he had a dream of a ship emerging from the sea-mist, a long low craft with rowers amid-ships, a single mast and great square purple sail embroidered with a great crimson dragon. And there, sitting in a carven chair high on the stern poop with a great book in her lap was the woman who became the troubling of his life.

He told it well, I will give him that - far better than I could have done. Then again Ethel told me that he spent a lot of time during the War writing anonymous pacifist poems and articles for socialist journals and often got damned by some of his readers for using the word 'bloody' too often. Yet his description of the woman with her long, dark hair like sea-weed in the tide, her pale face and scarlet lips and strange sea-goddess eyes clearly throbbed within him like the after-humming of great bells. I remember his words exactly:

'I looked at her and she looked at me', he wrote, a sigh in every word. But that was where he was wrong.

He was wrong because this uncanny woman was looking beyond his scrawny self to the man who *had* summoned her. His beloved Sea Priestess from the land beyond sunset, who would require many sacrifices for her goddess in order to save the land from drowning, only had eyes for the man standing right behind him.

She was looking at the man who was her eternal Earth Priest.

She was looking at *me*...

As for the 'land beyond sunset', she was actually from South Wales, as the great red dragon on the ships sail told everyone. The house 'Miss Morgan' had bought at the very tip of Brean Down looked directly across the Bristol Channel to Barry Island, perhaps 6 miles away. I had cannon during the War that could fire that far, looping over the murderous 40-foot tides that were higher and faster than others anywhere else in the world, with the fat conger and the wrecked boats and the lost souls of drowned mariners with eels in their skulls.

Yet his vision *was* a true one, for I was a part of it in ways he would never realise. I only wondered what dark magic Miss Morgan was about to work now, and what malefic tides she was about to influence in this quiet little humdrum backwater of souls.

Maxwell kept a diary, of which he was rather proud. I know that because he later used large parts of it in that ghost-written book I mentioned. I also know because Scottie showed it to me when his partner was away valuing, or being an expert witness for some local trivia.

The contents were pitiful: the excitements of a man who had never really lived except within his own mind and who had never quite grown up. The fact is, he was what was then known as a 'dope addict'. There were a lot of them about in those days, in his particular upper middle-class strata of Englishness with its lower upper-class pretensions. They were largely people with more money than sense, brainy in their own blinkered ways and highly strung. Even he blamed his schooldays for this, with the high precepts in the classrooms but unbelievably low practises in the dormitories. We all know what he meant by that. This was all perfectly legal then – the drug taking I mean, not the 'low practices' - but after the Dangerous Drugs Act these addicts became known in the popular mind as Drug *Fiends* after a best-selling novel of the time.[4]

Scanning through the pages that Scottie highlighted with his stubby, nicotined finger, the word 'dope' appears on almost every one. It was clear that he had been a user long before the first asthma attack. If indeed that was what it was.

I will admit that Miss Morgan made a clever choice when she bought those buildings at the tip of Brean Down. Out there, at either side and directly before, she could hear the endless contending voices of the land, sea and its tides that mirror those which move our souls. It was and is a powerful place and always will be, no matter how much it gets built around by the crass needs of humans in caravans and the holiday camps of the modern world. It stretches north-west for a mile and half and is 318 feet high, though it feels much more than that when you are on top and the wind howls.

Best of all, it is made of Carboniferous Limestone containing fossils that have been dated to 350 million years ago. Rock so solid that I could have fired shells from my biggest, Boche-destroying cannons and howitzers without the recoils crumbling the world underfoot and actually increasing the range because of this firmness. Don't remind me of the noxious, smelly mud I had to deal with in Flanders that caused so many misfires and misses. That sort of washed-out, watery, marshy landscape was just what Miss Morgan would have thrived on. I was often surprised I never saw her over there, but then she always did prefer to be hidden, diluted to our world if you like.

---

[4] This was probably 'Diary of a Drug Fiend' by Aleister Crowley.

And on the spine of this great hard penis (for that is how all the local saw it, a Great Dick, as I said) there were still the remains of lost and forgotten worship going back to the Bronze Age, fragments of Temples that tried to cap the up-flowing upsurges like a kind of gushing spiritual oil. There were prehistoric barrows heaving with ancestral souls, plus the remains of a 4th century Celtic Temple that was later turned into a Christian oratory to try and attune to or even tame the wilder energies.

Not a chance, I say.

And then there was the actual Fort that Miss Morgan had purchased[5]. It was built a nearly century before as part of a chain of defences across the Bristol Channel just in case that little chancer Napoleon III got uppity again and tried to emulate his glorious uncle. Said uncle, I would point out, was an artillery man through and through and owed his Empire to his cannons. He might have been the Nightmare of Europe but in another shape or form I could have served him right proudly. Perhaps there is a part of me across Time that actually did.

I could close my eyes and feel the energies spurting up from the Deep Time of inner earth, even through the thick soles of my old Army boots that we called 'Crunchies' because of the sound they made on gravel, and would last me a few years more.

Yes, I saw at once the attraction the Fort held for Miss Morgan. Especially that strange small structure she insisted on calling 'The Frenulum', perched on the very tip of this earth-prick. At high tide it would be surrounded by the waves like a Japanese temple I once saw pictures of; at low tide there would still be enough water at either side of the shaft for her Special Needs. She was – is – like a dolphin: an air-breathing mammal that needs the sea and its lunar currents. Whatever it was she had planned for this place, it would meet her purpose.

Weeks later, before my building for her was done, we paused and looked across to the north-west and a setting sun. I was willing to be cordial: Earth and Fire, Water and Air can and should balance. I pointed across with gnarled finger and told her:

God's own country the Welsh have always said.

She pursed her red lips. I could see why Maxwell was attracted, of course I could.

Young gods, I fancy. Can you row me there?

---

[5] Now under the benign aegis of the National Trust.

Fighting the currents, the cold dark and murderous waters of the Severn? They are too much like you.

She smiled. Not offended in the least. Nor had I meant offence: it was a simple statement.

I could fix you up with an old Army friend, we all nicknamed Merl – for Merlin. He'd be more suitable for whatever it is you're doing than this Mr. Maxwell.

Suitable?

He's the son of a steel-worker, slaughterer of the Boche, now studying to be a doctor, I heard.

She looked at me with her wide eyes, the irises entirely whole, now black as the waters of the Severn.

You cannot hypnotise me, 'Miss Morgan'.

I know that. Yet you would be annoyed if I did not try.

I do think she was hypnotising Maxwell with her uncanny eyes and deep, throaty voice and the unspoken but hinted promise that *if* he was good, if he was very *very* good, and *if* he met her special if unusual needs, then something amazing might happen to an ageing virgin like himself.

The man was making a complete fool of himself, and the dope didn't help. Ethel tried to tell him but he snarled at her. She tried to keep away his dealer, Beardmore, a seedy wretch who was an addict himself, a 'junkie' as they started terming them – addicts who would sell scrap metal and other junk to pay for their habit. I wondered if Beardmore had been involved in the removal of the smaller cannons that had disappeared mysteriously overnight from the Fort. One way or another, flowing in secret places, The Drip himself always found a way to connect with Beardmore and his needles and claimed the circumstances were *entirely* medicinal and how nasty people were to think otherwise. And if the dope didn't do for him, then the alcohol did, for he was rarely away from the tame pub known as *The George* whose wine waiter catered for all his needs in the back room.

His mother, apparently, lived in the spacious rooms on the uppermost floor of the huge house and kept well out of it, letting the servants do the living for her.

I will admit that Maxwell described the Fort well enough in his self-serving Journal, making comments about the bends on the road and the ups and downs and precipitous drops and the million rabbits before you got to the concrete of the forecourt and the old barracks and semi-circle of gun emplacements. And beyond them a long, narrow tongue of half-tide rock that shot into the water like a spurt from the prick. (I knew that the energies of this tongue interested his customer more than the buildings she had just bought.) He wrote – and this annoyed me – 'I thought of what life must have been like here for the God-damn Tommies' who lived in those cold barracks and toiled up there with their supplies before the days of motor lorries.

If he actually deigned to speak to me I could have told him... The Fort was originally staffed by 50 officers and men of the Coast Brigade, Royal Artillery and *I* had been one of those Tommies, though whether I was damned by his God was not for me to say.

Maxwell, you see, rarely spoke to me except to give orders. I was never more than one of his servants, paid to do some renovation. A handyman, carpenter and builder. Like so many men of his class he would have quite intimate conversations with his peers while his servants stood mutely in the background. Old Sally Sampson was one of these invisible souls who, serving them tea and cakes, had taken in every word of the vicious bickering between Wilfred, Ethel and their Mater known as The Dame, and repeated everything to everyone of her class in town. *Do they think we can't hear? Do they think we don't have opinions? Do they think we're just bits of furniture?* she quietly raged to me once. In the eyes of the Great Mother - the most senior of Maxwells - modern democracy was a dead dog and most people should be put back into slavery.

However... Ethel was a little different. In fact she had actually written a book called, I think, *The Psychology of the Servant Problem* that made her seem like a dangerous intellectual among the self-styled elite of Weston-super-Mare. As she worked through her own psychologies I think it allowed her to fall in love with my little Fleur despite the class gap. And also a little bit in love with me, too.

I had the best of both worlds in this context. Miss Morgan, who knew exactly who and what I was, would speak openly to Wilfred and didn't care that I was working away in earshot and listening to everything, every nuance, sensing the undercurrents in ways that Wilfred never could. In the odd ways in which she worked, everything she said was directed more to me than him.

And he never knew.

Or was even much aware of my existence.

I could have been one of the whispering spirits that Miss Morgan kept banging on about.

I was preparing all the materials, equipment and tools needed for the renovations she had outlined so very sketchily (as if she never intended anything permanent), when Scottie came to me in a state of some agitation. He had heard – without saying how - that Miss Morgan, under the name of 'Vivien le Fay Morgan', had spent a few seasons as an actress or a dancer or even worse – he wasn't sure which.

Did you confront your partner?

I showed Mr. Wilfred the front page of last week's Herald exposing nightclubs in London where people, 'mixed in race and manners' it said!!! - paid young women for... thriiiills.

He actually shuddered when he whispered that last word, Calvinist that he was. I tried not to smile.

And what did Maxwell say?

He just laughed. He told me, as if I was a complete idiot, it was no more than a 'provincial pantomime', in which she played the Demon Queen in a touring version of Jack and the Beanstalk. Well, she would say that wouldn't she? Aye, aye, he growled, jutting his jaw, then drawing on a cigarette before blowing out the smoke through narrow lips like an artillery piece himself.

Scottie was convinced that she was one of those Dope Girls that were in the newspapers of that time - young women of Chinese origin who brought drugs into Britain via the Bristol docks. With her almond eyes she could – almost - be mistaken as Oriental.

Perhaps he was right, I did not care, not then, not at first.

So I organised three good men and true to help me, and one of them really was called Bindling, so maybe that's where Maxwell got the name from. Mind you, by the time he paid for that American ghost-writer to tell his story, his brain was probably long addled by the drugs.

He wasn't *Old* Bindling though, being only half my age if that. They were all ex-Army and glad of the work during that time of mass unemployment in their Land Fit for Heroes. We hired a huge hay-cart with a couple of lush-haired old Clydesdales, with their towering height and genial nature, to pull it. I think they might have served on the Western Front also, pulling cannons for all their worth. We loaded it with all the gear I felt we would need: wheelbarrows, saws, sand and cement, bricks, plaster, hammers, screwdrivers, drills, toilet rolls, crowbars, nails and screws of every size by the bagful. Then we trundled out to the Fort via the Army road and its hair-pin bend with the sound of the sea below, gurgling and chuckling at the thought it might claim us.

Not a chance. Kaiser Bill couldn't. Brean Down wouldn't.

Miss Morgan had come up already in Maxwell's car - a Daimler would you believe. After the War the rest of us had fought, how could he have bought German? She stood watching our arrival and was wearing a loose blankety sort of coat of grey-green with a big, fluffy, upstanding collar of light-coloured fur. I could only just see her eyes over the top. In fact, I doubt if anyone had *ever* seen her face on the open street. Scottie reckoned this was because she was probably on Wanted posters all over Somersetshire, though I never did see any such things anywhere for anyone. That was Scottie for you. He lived an intense life inside his imagination. Some people might envy that.

Then her honeyed tones again:
Who are these men, Mr. Steele?
Tom, Dick and Harry, Miss Morgan.

I had to say that because they were all pretty leery about this strange project hers and didn't want to get sucked into any criminal undercurrents.

I could feel her smile behind the collar.
More like Shadrach, Meshach and Abednego.

Well, we all knew that story from our Infant School days, though few hear it now. You know how it goes, from the Book of Daniel... Shadrach, Meshach and Abednego were three young men determined to worship the One True God only, even if it meant their death. So they were thrown into the fiery furnace by the King of Babylon himself. Yet to his astonishment the flames did not touch them. And when he peered in, he sees a mysterious fourth person in there with them. So they won their freedom to worship Whoever, however they wanted.

No, Miss Morgan. Just *Tom, Dick and Harry.*

Then you must be the fourth person?

I shrugged. Our teacher in the Infants School at Brent Knoll made us draw pictures of the flames that we pinned on the walls of the class and he told us no-one in the Bible knew who the fourth person was; so how should I?

But will these Toms Dicks and Harrys survive the Fiery Furnace out **here***, Mr. Steele?*

They survived Passchendaele.

She had no answer to that.

No-one ever did. My lads did it for their own One True King and Country.

I detected a whiff of shame upon the sea air as the gulls ruffled above and made curving dives to the waters.

Are you a Daniel?

That **is** *my first name, Miss Morgan,* as she of all people in this world knew full well, though she didn't get the story quite correctly; I suppose she thought Daniel was the Unknown One, the fourth man and saviour to the three boys, whereas he was merely a magician to the King.

Or perhaps Miss Morgan knew more than I in this respect.

As it was my lads all took a fancy to Miss Morgan. Or as much of her as they could see, given her clothes. They wondered if she was 'loose', as all the gossip spread by Scottie throughout Weston insisted, and very much hoped so. You can take young men out of the Army but... You know the rest. We lost more men in our battalion to V.D. than from German shelling, but that was always hushed up[6]. I didn't have any bromide to put in their tea to keep the urges of this lot down: I didn't need to. Miss Morgan was more than able to fend for herself.

Although the War had ended four years before they still responded to the Army discipline and the fact that I had been a sergeant and they no higher than privates.

All right lads, let's get cracking...

---

[6] At one point 11,000 men were hospitalised with VD. That was entire infantry division.

Before I get drawn into and sucked down by the currents of Wilfred Maxwell's first vision of his 'Sea Priestess', I should say something about myself. If there is such a thing as this 'karma' that the Theosophists talk about, then perhaps balance – or holy forgiveness - might come from an understanding of me, and what I am.

I feel that I was born around 1880. I say 'feel' rather than 'know' because I was adopted. There was nothing official, no documents that I ever saw, no whispered histories or rumours or scandals surrounding me – would that there had been, so that I could truly 'Know Myself'! In a time of high infant mortality, the fact that someone took me on was no small act of mercy. The couple who did this was David and Mabel Carstairs who ran their small Abaris School on Eldon Way, at the edge of the village of Brent Knoll, at the foot of the Knoll itself.

According to them, when I was old enough to ask, I came from nothingness and nowhere. So I fancied that I must have come from across the Bristol Channel, perhaps born in one of the mystic Welsh valleys where men like dragons mined the black gold known as coal. Or perhaps it was merely Barry Island, that had once been ruled by a tribe known as the Silures. I suppose, as much as any other sort of identity, I am quite happy to think of myself as Silurian. I do like that word: *Si… lu…rian*. It slides over my tongue in the dark cave of my mouth and makes me think of dragons and earth-serpents.

I have no memories of my earliest moments, just a sense of me emerging from this darkness and nothingness and being looked at by an old bearded man and a woman next to him who radiated sorrow.

Whether these were my parents or simply the authorities who dumped me with the Carstairs I do not know.

Of course I *wanted* to know, and understand. Every orphan does. Although he adopted me, I always thought of Carstairs as 'The Father', because I never felt the sense of belonging that might make me utter that potent term 'Dad'. You can understand, perhaps, why my little Fleur's use of that name is a true Word of Power to my ears, more awesome than any of the cannon I fired in the Great War.

I asked 'The Father' several times about my origins:

Where did I come from, sir? Who named me Daniel Steele, sir?

But he only ever said, with a cheeky smile:

You just appeared! You just are – and always will be! You are what you are, ever-becoming.

My life before I arrived in Brent Knoll was like the chalk marks on the school blackboard after it had hurriedly been wiped.

He was a very clever man, Carstairs, always joking, who had a quick answer for everything else but he ducked and dived over this, his answers zig-zagging down into nonsense. Eventually I gave up asking. If I sound ungrateful I don't mean to be. He took me in and built me up from nothingness – he and the stick-thin somewhat distant figure I thought of as 'The Mother'. I think that she must have had mental problems as she rarely emerged from her upper rooms except to play piano in school assemblies with an angry, jabbing touch on the keys. I owe them, I really do. Is that what the Theosophists mean by karma? I won't ask any that I might meet. They all seem as wet as The Drip himself.

I noticed that the Carstairs rarely spoke to each other. There was no obvious hostility; they were more like the Punch and Judy puppets on the seafront at Weston, with him screeching *That's the Way to do it!*. Yet who was *their* puppet-master? I doubt if anyone could know.

So I grew up in the small village of Brent Knoll that stretched along the base of the Knoll itself, but never had more than a couple of hundred souls there during my years. The Knoll was an upsurge of the same rock and of the same height as Brean Down, less than three miles away. In terms of geology they were siblings, joined secretly in the dark under-earth between them, sending slow pulses to each other through the ages. Father Carstairs told me that Brent meant 'Beacon' and that Brent Knoll was a 'High Place' in the sense of something special and holy. I remember he gave his high-pitched laugh when he spoke of local belief that it had been created by the Devil! That seemed to tickle his fancy when he mimicked the Devil carving out Cheddar Gorge and then throwing a handful of the discarded rock out toward the sea that became the Knoll. I didn't see much funny in it myself. Maybe he saw more than I ever did.

When the classroom was too much for me I spent a lot of time on its slopes where people had worshipped in some way for the past 10,000 years according to the latest theories. There were the remains of walls – stone fragments - that had once been crude temples to forgotten gods and goddesses that I couldn't begin to name, but the stones seemed to thrum at me and I was often surrounded by the Misty Folk and the strange globs of light that seemed to be sentient, rising from the cracks in the ground as if to acknowledge me. Of course, the Romans poked their hooky noses here as everywhere and built their own short-lived fort with temple, calling it 'Mons Ranarum', which meant Isle of Frogs, I think, though I can't say I ever saw or heard one. I seem to remember a pond on the eastern side where I could peer into the waters where the Fays, as I thought of them, swam in their underworlds and tried not to evolve into humans. Or maybe I was just looking at tadpoles.

Oh – I almost forgot the swans! They arrived silently in early November and left in late February. Throbbing white clouds of them. Carstairs said they flew north taking the souls of the Brent Knoll departed with them. But I never quite connected with *those* Mysteries.

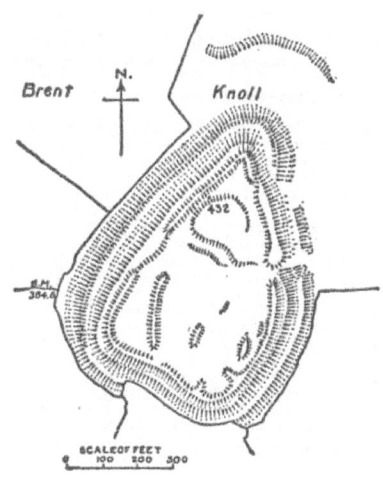

The Father told me of a local legend that one of King Arthur's knights, Sir Edern, son of Nudd, fought a great and final battle there with three giants. Carstairs went on to say that Nudd meant Darkness, or Old Night, and it seemed to my young self that being a Son of Darkness had a nobility about it that earthly titles could never match – although I did wonder about those Giants he fought. Were they Earth Giants, living at the deepest levels of Time and its perceptions below and within us? Or those long-skulled Old Folk who built the long barrows? I doubt if *they* were more than 6 feet tall, but in those days they would have seemed huge to the smaller people who took over everything and built round barrows.

Apart from that, many locals believed that this was the site of Badon itself, where King Arthur defeated the Danes – or was it the Saxons? – and King Alfred was believed to have stopped the Great Heathen Army there – or it could have been Cromwell routing the Cavaliers for all I knew. There was always a battle going on at some level. There was so much slaughter on the Knoll I think I took the essence with me when I went to the actual Land of Frogs. I knew that I would have to be a part of this someday, somewhere, because in my mind it was already happening, ever-becoming, here on the slopes of a seemingly modest Somerset hill.

For those of you who know your Thomas Malory, I also learned later (and it might have been Sir Edern himself who whispered it to me when the breeze was from the North) that Edern was the son Sir Uwaine le Blanchmaine. And that he, Uwaine, was the child of King Uriens and… Morgan le Fay! I might have been a bastard in terms of blood and breeding, but I was overshadowed throughout by the Queen of Crones herself. I was touched to learn, only recently, that one of my old pals from the Royal Field Artillery is buried in the church dedicated to St. Edern in Anglesey. One day I must visit.

It seemed to me that no matter how much I tried to avoid or evade 'my' Morgan, yet she was invisibly present in some way, whether directly here-and-now in the Fort, or indirectly on the Knoll during my childhood when I sat next to my twin sister Vivien in our special school. Was Morgan in my blood? Is she in everyone's blood? God help us every one.

Apart from the hill and all it contained on many levels of Time and Magic, there really wasn't much to the village itself beyond its Norman church (dedicated to St Michael who scares away demons), the old Red Cow pub, a Parish Hall, a Chapel that had been erected by the Bible Christian Society (in which The Father was sometimes asked to give awkward talks), and the small Church of England School that was quite separate from the one us abandoned waifs and strays attended.

The Knoll offered fine views for a rarity of tourists on a clear day... The glistening Polden Hills to the south, the Mendips with its Gorge and stalactite caves to the north, the Black Mountains of Wales to the far West and the upraised, reproaching finger of Glastonbury Tor to the east. As 'The Father' kept taunting the local vicar (who was a follower of Archbishop Ussher and the belief that Creation began in 5490 B.C.) people have lived around Brent Knoll and Brean for at least ten thousand years before the vicar's world supposedly began.

Yet in practice, no-one with any sense stayed for very long during Victorian times, because if the rhynes were not kept clear the land was regularly flooded. People in that area would have sleepless nights worrying about this.

Rhynes, I would explain, is a Somerset name for the drainage ditches or small canals used to turn areas of wetland close to sea-level into useful pasture. The area between Brean Down and Brent Knoll was a huge criss-cross of rhynes like the scars on the back of a flogged soldier. Even now, and probably for always, people were agitating about the need for rhynes to be kept clear, or repaired, or expanded in order to drain the land lest the sea come in, else they'd have another local apocalypse like the Great flood of 1872 when over 100 square miles of land were flooded and thousands drowned.

I have often wondered if that disaster had something to do with *my* origins.

So I grew up in this (outwardly) something-or-nothing place of Brent Knoll which I recognised immediately in Maxwell's book *The Sea Priestess* where it is disguised – very thinly and somewhat confusingly – as Bell Knowle.

I ran away from school, lied about my age to join the Army - and rarely looked back. Years later, during the Great War that I had always felt was my destiny, I heard the most bizarre rumour that David Carstairs had lied about his age too – but in reverse! I don't know how old he must have been, but he joined up in 1914 and commanded one of those Bicycle Battalions that were formed to cause havoc behind the German lines when they were breached. They never did get going. He apparently died in Flanders during one of their Big Pushes.

I will never understand the man. Once, much later, standing at the Tomb of the Unknown Warrior in Westminster Abbey, I was sure it was him in there.

As I said, the older I get, the more I realise how much I owe him.

So... that's me in a nutshell. Or instead of a 'nutshell' do I mean the spent shell of a cannon, reeking marvellously of cordite?

But all praise where it is due, the prose of Dope Fiend Maxwell made Brent Knoll *glow*. Yet I doubt if he ever went there except briefly, when he was out valuing properties or doing his side-line in antiques of unknown provenance and dubious origin.

I suppose you could describe me in those terms too.

Yet I must credit him with being a kind of fire-lighter in his writing: Like everything else, he took he took a very ordinary place and situations and puffed them into something brighter, more luminous, like blowing on dull embers – unless it was that ghost-writer of his who managed this.

Or perhaps it was all down to the dope that I saw him taking every day out at the Fort when we started work there.

I was certainly going to stop that in my own earthy way. I wouldn't be wishy-washy.

If Maxwell's prose was luminous when describing Bell 'Knowle', then it got even brighter and more intense when he described what happened after his 'Sea Priestess' first arrived in his mind. I know that we can all have such dreams: moments when a face can make the world stop and your heart pause at the top of its beat and one of the tectonic plates in your life shifts. That's when you get tremors that usually resolve themselves. Sometimes, though, it develops into a full quake.

In his Journal he wrote about the foreign high-prowed boats in the harbour he called Ishtar's Beere, though I've no idea where he got *that* name. And about the dark, far-travellers with curled beards and gold rings giving way to the armed men who had been expecting her, and who looked to him like a gathering of Chieftains. These, locals and land-lubbers, were rubbing shoulders uneasily with the shaven-headed priests the sea-priestess had brought with her to unleash her terrible human sacrifices that would control the floods. I was surprised, and a little impressed, that real terror comes through his prose as he describes these priests: their shaven, pallid, 'parchment faces' with cold, lashless eyes and cruel, resolute lips who were accustomed to terrible things in a terrible cult that would sacrifice young men who had 'never known women'. He described it better than that, and in some depth, but that is the nub.

What struck me – annoyed me actually - was the phrase he used: *'Never known women'*. That was something I noticed throughout his Journal: he was afraid to use the word 'virgin'. *Never known women...*

That was Wilfred Maxwell himself of course, in his own words, and it was almost a boast intended to conceal. I am quite sure he had 'known men' in his boarding school days, as he had hinted when he mentioned the 'unbelievably low practises in the dormitories'. Why else had he never, at the age of 35, even come close to 'knowing' a woman - even though by his own estimation he was the most eligible bachelor in and around Weston-super-Mare!? He despised the town. He described it to Scottie (who repeated it to me with some shock) that he saw it as a filthy place, all asphalt and lodging houses and pierrots in the summer and wind in the winter and the ignorant, narrow people - an even worse breed than the Welsh who came over in the ferry at weekends. His words.

What did he ever know? He spent endless hours in *The George,* where he had something going with the wine-waiter that probably involved drugs, and was known around all the local towns as an alcoholic. He saw Weston as a mud-encroached dump inhabited by dead-end people in total decline.

How blind...

With my own Two Sights – inherited from god-knows who – I knew that the local farriers on Drove Road were actually centaurs who kept to their own kind and were quite lordly toward the rest of us. I knew of the swift, white-blooded creatures akin to unicorns in the Weston Woods, and their guardians - who not entirely physical. And also of several secretive families who worked as coppicers who were goat-footed. Not to mention the dragon folk, the Cymry, who flapped their ancient, leathery atmospheres around themselves like wings. 'Vivien le Fay Morgan', as she styled herself, may have seduced Wilfred Maxwell by claiming to be a Sea Priestess from a far-away land, but there were any numbers of these beings around. You didn't need the Two Sights to understand what lies beneath *any* town – just a willing heart and a deep sense of touch.

I noticed in his ghost-written book (which is hugely indiscreet if you knew the man himself) that he got quite aroused wearing Miss

Morgan's nightclothes when she wasn't looking, prancing around her bedroom when she was away. My lads were to see him wearing her apricot-coloured dressing gown with swansdown fluffers, spraying himself madly with her expensive perfumes, but they said nothing and walked away to lay more concrete in a foundation.

Each to his own, I say, but the point is, he described the meeting in which I – or a part of me - had been present when we had welcomed – reluctantly - the sea-priestess from what he came to fancy was Atlantis. Not so, Wilfred Maxwell. She simply came from the *true* Avalon in South Wales. It was never that place with the pointing finger to the east of Brent Knoll, but you have to blame the later graspingly devious monks of Glastonbury for that sort of myth-thievery.

And his prose – or did the *ghost-writer's* own vision take over!? – then looked into the large cave under the hill where there was a welcoming feast around a High Table and scraps flung to the dogs beneath it. He described the tensions between our bearded uneasy warriors and the shaven headed parchment-skinned priests with faces like white conger eels and the rugged, bronzed King between them, trying to balance things but wishing that the tribes – fractious as the land - had listened to him for once. And then Maxwell spoke about the great bowl that they brought, carved with the waves of the sea and the Moon in its phases and all manner of strange sea-creatures.

But... *I* didn't see it that way. It was not a carven wooden bowl but a silver cauldron, decorated with boar and dogs and dragons and fighting men and stags and trees and their entwining roots and everywhere the symbols in homage to the Horned God whom I served and still serve.

So that was me. *I* was The King under the Hill, hoping to see the last of this sea-priestess and her useless sacrifices. I never saw the point of them, but my clan was desperate. *Dig and channel*, I told them, *channel and dig deep into the land, drain the land, work the land using rock and stone to create small walls that will channel the flow of water back into the sea* – and create what they would call in a thousand years' time *rhynes*.

My people didn't want to listen, or do the work. They just had to sacrifice a few useless fellows, as they insisted the 'Sea Priestess' had promised, and they'd be saved. Slaves that no-one would miss. The same sort of people used much the same sort of sacrifices or offerings in 1914 when a whole generation was drowned in the mud of Flanders to save the Land and its Peoples.

And then there was his memory of tricking his awesome 'Sea Priestess' into having sex: Taking his virginity before she drowned him as one of the holy and Willing Sacrifices that were all the rage in those days.

Did they have sex? I doubt it. This sea-borne woman, this 'Morgan' (for that is what the name means), probably drugged him stupid and left him chained in the sea-cave for the cold waves to claim him so she could get on with the *real* business of her visit...

She was not there just to control the Waters; she sailed across the bitter, dirty waters of the Channel to mate with the King – *me* - as part of an ancient pattern of life and death, ebb and flow, giving and taking that made perfect sense at the time. Her first whispered words to me after she had drowned the nuisance who would become Wilfred were literal, and not symbolic, and would have been said in Ancient Egypt between the Pharaoh and his wife:

Hello brother. Shall we begin...?

Oh, in a troubling echo in a later Age, 'Miss Morgan' out on Brean Down had Wilfred like a fish on a string and no-one could have unhooked him. He just spun and spun in secret agony that wasn't *all* to do with the dope. Have you ever, as a landsman, tried removing a fish-hook– or a piece of twisted shrapnel - from your flesh? The only way is to push the hook in further, creating more pain, until it curves and breaks through to the surface where you can pull it through and out. That was what Miss Morgan did to Mr Maxwell.

I am not a 'reincarnation', as the Theosophists would think of it. At least I don't think I am. It's more that I am a pulse in Time, a continuation of Earth energies. Strike a tuning fork – the next one responds.

But I must describe the work we did out at the Fort. Have I told you that it was a rugged building that he wanted to transform into something arty-farty and otherworldly? It was a British Army Fort, built to withstand extremes of weather, French cannon (the French were renowned for their artillery) plus the slow, brutal abuses caused by squads of frustrated Tommies who were barracked there at what must have seemed like a big white asylum perched the end of the civilised world. Some of them went mad.

There was no glass left in any windows or any door on its hinges and we immediately had to fish numerous dead birds and other decayed creatures out of the water tanks. Maxwell wrote that this had been no more than a single jackdaw, but he never came near us workers so how could he know? Besides, despite his expensive education, I doubt if he knew a jackdaw from a squirrel.

We got the water running and ran flue-brushes up the various chimneys or fired them with old newspapers in the old-fashioned way, so that they eventually hissed and snarled like one of the old Stokes Mortars used on the front lines and sent flames roaring upward into the Somerset skies.

Inside, in the block that Miss Morgan had earmarked as her main dwelling, Maxwell beavered away seeking to curry favour or win praise or whatever it is that his sort felt they had to do in their relationships with women. We caught glimpses of him with smuts on his face from black-leading the old cast-iron fireplaces, and he always paint on his fancy clothes from some vast mural he was working on to cover the blank white internal walls. If Love required Labour he was only interested in the pretty-pretty stuff and not the hard effort that ordinary people have to use.

As for us, he was barely aware of us except out the corner of his eye, making sure that Miss Morgan (when she was not doing mysterious things in London), did not get near me. Or me near her. Although my lads worked hard, like many an officer (though not all) he rarely came near us on the front lines.

Yet for some reason he became obsessed with the hair-pin bend on the road up to the Fort. He seemed to see symbolism in it: as though the route from Earth to Heaven was unnecessarily twisted and dangerous and needed to be made straight. If you ask me it was *him* that was twisted and dangerous.

That, he ordered into the air to one side of me, *had to be dealt with.* I fancy he almost expected me to answer *Yes sir!* Of course I wouldn't, ever, never, couldn't. I didn't care what work we did as long we were paid by the week, cash in hand, in advance. I knew from Scottie that the business was always one cheque away from disaster so I had to look after my lads in this way. That was my kind of Love and its Labour, mock how you want.

Although the gradient was 1 in 4 the 'hair-pin bend' wasn't very hair-pinny or bendy at all, not like the long and murderous one further along the coast at Porlock. I'd had more difficult tasks in Flanders when the real danger was not one of falling off a cliff, but of our huge cannon sinking into the mud until only its muzzle showed like the O of a goldfish's mouth. Then there would be hell to pay from our Colonel and we'd need teams of huge horses (any breed) from other units, plus dozens of men (any regiment) to haul it out before we got spotted by the Boche with their binoculars in the tethered balloons or Richtofen's Circus flyers sending our coordinates across the lines so we we got their monstrous shells upon us. Though sometimes the ground around us was so soft that their shells didn't explode and we lived to shit again, as we said.

That was the only time I ever found a use for mud.

Which causes me to ask what might seem like a stupid question, although even as I say this I'm reminded of dear Mr Carstairs - my 'Father' who is now in Heaven – who often said quite firmly: *There is NO SUCH THING as a stupid question, dear boy*. So... what caused the mud? I have to ask. Well, water of course. That is obvious, I know, but I have to say it because I saw in Maxwell's *Journal* a comment that the sea-born Morgan made: how sacrificing humans to the Water was **necessary** and **logical** because the sea would always be senior.

No, no NO... that was an argument I always had with her. There is no such thing as a world made entirely of water – unless you count raindrops as a 'world'. Water needs the hard core of rock and fire. There must be billions of worlds that exist without water – huge orbiting lumps of rock/earth/stone and fire, but none that exist as water alone. Sea Priestesses have no substance. They swirl, create pools or swamps and always evaporate.

Jealous jealous jealous was her usual ridiculous response. *You really should grow up, Daniel.*

The Sea Priestess and I have had this argument times without number, aeons and worlds without end, a to-ing and fro-ing that was almost like sex itself. Out at the Fort, almost in passing, energies flowed from me to her and her to me that were entirely sexual, and yet we never touched, not with flesh. There on Brean Down, with her sideways glances at me, her smiles and secretly blown kisses when Maxwell's back was turned, I wondered if she was even human any more.

So we dealt with the bend and left him and Miss Morgan when she was here to their devices - playing with a large crystal, as my lad Tom told me, all agog. *Each to their own Tom*, I said, though of course that wasn't his real name at all. Every now and again we would hear Maxwell's hyena laugh that was so much like a strangled seagull and we would pause, smile, then carry on into the earth-workings.

They were often arguing and there were moments when I saw a strange dark turmoil in his eyes. Almost the look of someone drowning. It was never an equal to-and-fro between them although Maxwell tried his best. He was more used to shouting down and occasionally slapping his sister in order to win an argument - he wouldn't dare try that against Miss Morgan. I also heard him confessing to her to being a bit of a masochist. I had to ask Scottie what that was. He furrowed his white eyebrows and looked it up in a dictionary of the new-fangled 'psychology' that Maxwell had on his writing desk.

We looked at each. We nodded. That made sense.

Sand Fairy Ann[7] I concluded, using the phrase picked up in France. Being an Army chap himself he nodded.

But I ramble…

It was on a fine afternoon when the bend had been straightened and the land fixed and my lads stood around in their braces and khaki trousers, smoking short pipes, when who did we see but Beardmore on his motorcycle. His rubbery face seemed to have collapsed below his bayonet nose. Blood dripped from one nostril onto the long, oil-skin coat that covered his fat belly, like a seal.

I stood in the middle of the narrow road.

I'm bringing Mr. Maxwell his medicine.
If you say so, I replied, though I didn't care to step aside.
He will become very ill if he doesn't take it.
So you say.
He needs it.
So you say. But does he? Does he really?

---

[7] 'Ça ne fait rien' – meaning 'never mind' or 'it doesn't matter'

I was tempted to give him one firm push on his left shoulder and man and machine would have plummeted to the rocks a hundred feet below. Then we'd see if his seal coat and fat belly would help him swim

Tom must have sensed this. He hadn't been a soldier for nothing.

Mr. Steele... he said, no more than that, yet those two words made me human again.

You're not a doctor, Beardy.

But I'm a specialist.

Where do you get this medicine?

It's imported. From a Mongolian with his international office in Bristol.

I was to learn from Maxwell's private *Journal* that the dealer was actually Tibetan (which seemed to justify everything in Maxwell's mind) and worked from a seedy little office rental on the Bristol Docks. Which just about confirmed Scotties early suspicions about the Chinese 'Dope Girls' that the newspapers raged about. Miss Morgan even sent him scurrying up there to buy what *she* said were little packets of sandal-wood done up like kindling to burn the Fires of Azrael, whatever they were, in lieu of actually having sex with him. 'They were not cheap' he moaned, and the fool wondered who actually burnt this expensive wood. Well, no-one did. They were packets of heroin, of course. He must have known that. By the time his *Journals* were transformed by his ghost-writer into a full book, the 'Dangerous Drugs Act' had been passed, so I suppose he felt inclined to be a bit more cautious in what he said lest he face criminal charges.

But that word 'Mongolian' made me bristle again. It was almost an attack on Fleur. I made an instant calculation about his likely trajectory if he had been a shell from one of my low-angled massive field howitzers.

Mr Steele... said Tom again, touching my arm, a very human pressure and a very kind pressure. Soldiers who have killed understand this. I stood aside to let the wretch past.

There is a darkness in your heart, Sarge, whispered Tom, who still used my rank.

Fat bastard, muttered Dick.

Wally Walrus said Harry, and made *arf arf* noises like a seal.

I learned what was going on in Maxwell's mind on almost a daily basis. This was because to save money he ran his estate agent's business in part of the very large house in Weston in which the Maxwell family lived. Scottie, who never had many real scruples when it came to protecting the business (even if he did shiver and shake at his boss's cavorting with Miss Morgan), peeked into Maxwell's private diary whenever the man left the building. And every morning when I came to leave Fleur with Ethel before I went to work at the Fort, and also afterward to pick her up when I had finished, he showed me, his eyes huge with shock behind his steel-rimmed glasses.

Scottie, in fact, was as Scottish as me. That is, probably not at all. Why he affected a pseudo-Scottish accent I do not know. Everyone needs to have their own secrets and quirks, and I have more than most. Weston's pork butcher, Muckley by name and nature, whispered that Scottie had been a deserter during the war: that he had hidden out in the witch-ridden Welsh Marches and changed his identity when it was over. I shrugged. Muckley made up tales that were are rotten as some of his products. He probably suspected that Scottie was that most perverted of all Westonians – a vegetarian. I didn't care what Scottie was or what he presumed to be, and he seemed to sense that. It must have been my kind face that made him trust me with the diary.

The actual entries were often quite minimal, and I suppose it was left to the ghost-writer to expand upon these in the eventual book. Sometimes they were almost indecipherable when the dope obliterated him as firmly as any shell blast. But there was enough to see into his mind, and keep watch and guard for what the 'Sea Priestess' might be doing to him and the business.

Thus after a day's hard work with Tom, Dick and Harry it was my delight to pick up and Fleur and see her offerings. I knew that I would have to absorb every moment as people like her were often prone to chest infections and did not live long. As if they weren't cursed enough! She would never get accepted for infant school anyway, so Ethel was a god-send.

I was surprised by how delicate Ethel's rooms were, that occupied most of the ground floor at the rear of the grand house. In Wilfred's *Journal* she comes across as a bit of a Tartar (do people still say that?) but her walls were a delicate pink-grey, with rush matting on some of the floors and old, silky Persian rugs on others. I knew these were 'Persian' because my late wife had a thing about carpets and we bought several at a bargain price when the Royal Pier Hotel went bust. There were paintings on the walls – originals I supposed – by Lawrence H. Davidson, of forests and glades and one large picture of a dormant but still smoking volcano. Near the sofa and by the fire she had a sturdy table on which Fleur's finger-painting and potato prints of the day were displayed. Logs were burning in the yellowed marbled fireplace of the sitting room and on another occasion, I might have fancied spending hours just staring into the fire-caves between the logs where the djinns danced. These were my elements, you understand.

Given the sour descriptions of Ethel in her brother's *Journal*, and scathing comments about the Friendly Girls (he really didn't like them) these were not the sort of rooms you would imagine she would inhabit: they were feminine, delicate, even. Then again, what did Wilfred Maxwell, a closet homosexual really know about women? And what choice did Ethel ever have in her own life, here at the edge of world in Weston-super-Mare, in an era when the Great War had obliterated a whole generation of marriageable men?

Fleur showed me the finger-paintings they had done, Ethel made a great show of mounting one of them on the wall, next to the posh paintings. Fleur glowed. So did I.

One day, Mr. Steele, there will be a civilization based on the Mysteries of Touch, and all that means; a field of consciousness which hasn't yet opened into existence – but we're much too afraid of it – we are stiff as this wood! she said, throwing another log on the fire.[8]

There were sparks of all kinds in the hearth at that moment.

You do all this and organise the Friendly Girls.

And I drink brandy. And gamble. And am handy with a twelve-bore, though I no longer go to grouse shoots.

I didn't know what to say. I understood she was making a pass at me, and I wasn't about to stop her.

You're like that painting there, Mr. Steele – like a volcano. Full of queer rumblings.

That's echoes of cannon fire, Miss Maxwell.

Ethel.

---

[8] Ethel seems to be quoting almost word for word from the first draft of the stolen manuscript 'Tenderness' by D.H. Lawrence.

Ethel. And I am Daniel.
Hello Daniel…

I was quite sure that Wilfred Maxwell would one day go mad – probably when he realised that 'Miss Morgan' was not quite what she seemed. The Fort was a perfect place for this to happen – the madness, I mean. That's what happened to my first Captain out there, though it may have been down to his experiences in the Boer War.

He seemed to like me and so taught me, a mere squaddie, everything about cannons. In the Fort's heyday it used to have three 7" rifled muzzle-loading guns. That dates me I suppose: there are people emerging who don't know what 'rifled muzzle-loading' even means, and the Army even now is describing its ordnance in the French style in millimetres. Each gun weighed 7 tons and had a 30-pound charge of gunpowder able to fire a 112-pound Palliser shot at 1,560 feet per second. This could pierce 8 inches of armour at 1,000 yards. It is enough to say that while 7" might be a paltry distance when scratched as a line along the ground, as the internal diameter of a cannon's barrel it is quite monstrous in its power. (The Fort also had a large, underground, gunpowder magazine filled with shells, 15 by 18 feet and 20 feet high. I didn't know it at the time, but this hidden space came to obsess both Maxwell and Miss Morgan.)

My Captain infected me with a love for these brutes. In fact, he spoke of all the cannons in the Fort as though they were his girlfriends – though I doubt if he actually had one: *That one needs coaxing; this one is sleek and willing; the one next to her flatters to deceive but you won't get far and she never offers up much; and that one there, she is just dirty, old and with a useless crack.* Then one morning for parade he didn't appear, and they wondered if he'd been caught in a rip-tide. I heard whispers that he saw things in the night. They said that he might have weighted his pockets with shells and jumped

He too was cracked….

On a day when Maxwell lay blotto on his couch after Beardmore had stuck enough dope into him to floor one of the Clydesdales and then drove off on his motorcycle, I stood at the very tip of the 'Dick' with 'Miss Morgan'. She wore a long, flowing dress of wine-coloured velvet, the big wing-sleeves looped back to her shoulders and showing a silvery lining. Her nails were a scarlet 'whore's claws' as Maxwell himself described them in his Journal, oozing with excitement.

We stood inside the Frenulum for which she had big plans and lavish drawings of queer sea beasts and sea plants, though to me it was no more than a squarish concrete box open to the front and rear that had once held a very large searchlight. The tide was at its uttermost ebb but I knew it would turn soon and the floating weeds long as Miss Morgan's hair in its oily dark waters, would soon flow in our direction. We had to stand shoulder to shoulder, as the space was limited. Things passed between us: part of the arcane and silent Mysteries of Touch. I had forgotten how attractive she was. She sighed.

It feels so pure here...

Pure? Her sea was not pure. It was dark mud with the effluent discharges from Bristol and Cardiff and a dozen smaller towns whose sewers poured their shit into the flow and whose Mayors hoped that somewhere along the line the mighty Atlantic would somehow purify it all. The source of this curving River Severn was 200 miles away, splurging up from a peat bog in Plynlimon amid the mountains of Wales, and marked by nothing more special than a wooden post. I wondered if I went there and removed that post that she would dissolve.

Wilfred is very poorly.

She was matter of fact about his poorliness.

My lads had already been paid and so I had not the slightest concern as to whether The Drip lived or died. He could be in his room screaming in agony and it would mean nothing to me. I still fought a Great War in my mind and had seen *real* men die in their thousands and been surrounded by their body parts. And I had killed tens of thousands of the enemy with my artillery. I said nothing. She read my every thought with her silken telepathy

It has been a long time, Daniel.
Not long enough.
You disapprove of my relationship with Wilfred?
I do not care. He is in the grip of your many fantasies.
What fantasy is that?
He thinks you're a Sea Priestess.
You know full well, I **am** *a Sea Priestess.*
In your own head.
Can she exist anywhere else?
You are a phoney.
No more than you.
I am Earth and Fire. Solid. The script of the stones. Eternal.
And I am the tongue of the wave. Rhythmic. I can be a phoney **and** *a Sea Priestess. If I ceased to believe in myself I think I would evaporate. I* **must** *believe in myself. Besides, I am transforming him.*
Into an addict.
He already was. Are you are deliberately forgetting the first time you and I met? Are you afraid of what we are?
Were.
You were always jealous of me. Remember what Carstairs kept telling us: 'Everything that can happen does happen'.

I went silent. She was very clever with words. I would feel swamped when I tried to argue. But she was right. I had tried to bury the memory of that first Impulse, that repeating pattern in Time in which she had come to Brent Knoll to mate with me, King of the Hill.

She put her hand on my shoulder. A woman's touch. Silence. Kindness. I had forgotten how much she attracted me, yet must always be forbidden.

You **are** *a phoney Viv. And* **I** *have changed. Transformed* **my** *Self.*
What would Carstairs say about us?

I should explain…

She had been found slightly later than me, but never quite took to our couple of Adopting Saviours and never used my term 'The Father' to relate to him. When he was in lecture mode, which was often, she once accused him of thinking he was 'Bloody Socrates', to which he replied cheerily without missing a beat: *Perhaps I am!* To her, he was always simply 'Carstairs', as if he were little better than a servant to be summoned. She would often say:

Look, Carstairs, I will do what I wilt.

And so you wilt, and so you wilt... was his inevitably cheery reply. Looking back, I see that he was always cheery, with the fixed smile of a doll.

He tried to get us to 'bond', as I think they started calling it, by saying that *actually* we were Biological Twins. He said those words 'Biological Twins' as though he were a High Priest in the Holy of Holies in his temple whispering the Divine Name into nothingness.

I liked Vivien, I really did. We did well in class together, learning as normal children do. If I was taken by the Old Testament story of Daniel, she couldn't get enough about the mention of Melchizadek. I never did find out why.

Although I should say something about that school...

In the village itself there was a small Church of England School for all the locals and also one for Catholics in Burnham – the small town disguised as 'Starber' in Maxwell's book. And there was ours... the Abaris School, a bland, anonymous structure with high surrounding walls of grey stone, tucked away in a sort of *cul de sac* off Eldon Way. I had heard the whole place had burned down some years after I left, presumably by some unhappy pupil or parent. I didn't learn until quite recently that it had been for 'special' children, if that's the right term. It was actually Scottie who explained this to me with his dying-to-be-shocked whispers, having no idea that I had been a graduate of sorts. Looking around in his office in all directions lest any of the Maxwells' servants might be ear-wigging, he told me that the county of Somersetshire in those days, with its marshes and poverty and remote and isolated communities, had issues with the usual bestiality involving sheep that all farming types warned about, but also with incest – usually father and daughter, mother and son, brother and sister. The children resulting from these had what might be called 'problems' he said, making screwing gestures at his temples. Perhaps that's where I got it into my head about me and my twin Vivien and the dangers of any progeny from her.

Surrounded by these awkward and unwanted children in our small and odd school and knowing nothing else, I took them all to be the norm. They were totally harmless, but there was no-one I could be 'best friends' with when I was growing up and inward. Except for my tiny daughter Fleur, I still haven't got such a creature now, despite years among the 'normal' people. Besides, during those short years I was getting a different sort of education when I went out on the Knoll among the Misty People and the fays and all those beings I suppose the Theosophists would call 'Elementals'. I learned that there was a bewildering realm within the Land that led me toward the stars.

Vivien told me, before she absconded forever, that – *actually* - most of the children were offspring of Royalty and this is where most of the funding for the school came from. She copied Carstairs with that insert - *actually* – so his teaching wasn't entirely wasted.

As I recall, like peering into a glass darkly, as the poet said, I have a dim memory of her muttering something about the possibilities of blackmailing 'The Nobs' as she called them, when she grew up. I would have just nodded. To me, she was an Idiot in her own right, or at best a Drama Queen as Mrs Carstairs once said.

She was never backward in coming forward and rarely stopped talking. There might be a term for that in the dictionary of new-fangled 'Psychology'. She had a wild eye for colours and shapes in that black-and-white era and was always dressing up, often stealing clothes from 'The Mother' - or 'Mrs Carstairs' as she coldly called the woman, becoming all sorts of characters within the dormitory or classroom, and practising ventriloquism that she learned from a tuppeny pamphlet from the Joke Shop on the new Pier in Weston. I was a pretty strange creature myself, I suppose, and didn't know how to relate to *anyone*. I might have taken to her properly as my twin sister but one day she simply disappeared.

Carried off by gypsies, as 'The Mother' whispered, without concern, glad to see the troublesome, argumentative back of her, always knowing everything and always having the last word. I actually wondered if she *had* been sold to gypsies. At that time, in parts of rural Dorsetshire and deepest Somersetshire also, men could still sell their wives quite legally. That Thomas Hardy fellow wrote about it somewhere.

As for the school, it must have closed when Carstairs was called to the War. Goodness knows what happened to the children, though no doubt Royalty would secretly look after their own. I wish they still had some place like it for my Fleur to attend, as she is the friendliest little thing you could wish to meet.

I never did find out the truth about where 'Vivien Morgan' really went. Yet here she was now, on the tip of Brean Down as the tide began to turn and the weeds in the grey-black, turgid waters started curving and twisting and waving toward us.

Come and see Wilfred's murals now that he's unconscious.

He doesn't want me to see them. He's afraid of me.

Many men were, I can be a jagged shaft of granite. He was probably afraid that me or my lads would fathom how he had escaped the War. Tom felt that he might have been a Conchie – that is Conscientious Objector. I had known a few – Quakers some of them - who had volunteered as stretcher bearers rather than take up arms. I had nothing by respect for *them*. They had it worse than any of the lads who chose to use their rifles or machine-guns to kill the Hun. On the other hand, Dick felt that Maxwell had been discovered in an act of buggery with some Colonel from a posh regiment – probably the Horse Guards or Household Cavalry. Harry felt certain he was a Freemason, the 'son of a widow' as he kept telling people, and that the funny handshake and rolled-up trouser leg saved him from conscription. There was a lot of that Masonic nonsense around then.

*It's not **fear**, he feels when he looks at you. That's why he looks away.*

I've seen his paintings, 'Miss Morgan'. They're mad. All those sea creatures. It's the dope talking.

The Soma, to be exact. Perhaps it is. But then again, he's an artist and you're not. He has a wonderful, almost spiritual eye for colour, for shape, for movement of line and intent. He's a true visionary.

That made me angry.

*During the Battle of Messines I achieved the greatest rate of fire in the British Army, sending 48 rounds in 75 seconds over a range of 6000 yards, and destroyed a dozen of their gun emplacements. My artillery positioning and tactical deployment was described, even by Boche prisoners, as deadly art-forms in their own right. Am **I** not an artist? What did your boyfriend ever do in the War?*

Actually... he's not a boyfriend. I don't know what he did, I was not in this country, I was in South America, believe it or not. I don't know or need to know - or judge. I'm sure he served in some way. Infantry?

*It was an **artillery** war, 'Miss Morgan' – that was the battle winner. I caused the greatest loss of life, the most dreadful of wounds and the deepest fear. I drove men to madness that caused them to pray for death. I'm not proud of that, but it won us the War. Are you going to drive Maxwell to madness?*

That's a strange sort of boast, Mr. Steele. Let's not argue...

As we walked back a wave made a dead-set at her ankles and she slipped on the rocks. It might have been deliberate. I grabbed her – I had to - and we were face to face and body to body and human warmth flowed through me as well as her wonderful perfume She saw my eyes, saw into me, and smiled. And I saw again that Time before the Times when the sea waves were mariners with gold ear-rings and curled beards, and the Spirits of Air that serve her formed as shaven-headed spiteful priests, while the Earth Spirits became the wary bearded warriors serving me, the King of the Hill. My thoughts rippled back and forward like the incoming tide and I did not know Who or What I was during the crests and troughs of this flow. Did we have to mate for the sake of our tribes this time? Would there be a new kind of sacrifice?

Oops! Very dimpsey today, Mr. Steele, she said in that bell-like tone, and somehow those innocent words and that wide-eyed expression offered me a glimpse into a treasure-box of images that would tempt the soul of any man. I couldn't do anything because the lads were watching everything, especially to see if I had a stiffy. You can take the boys out of the Army, but... you know the rest. I remembered a time in class when we were very young and Carstairs gave us two very large flat magnets. He showed us how the Like Poles repelled and the Unlike Poles snapped the two slabs together so tightly it was hard to pry them apart. With Vivien then, and at this moment decades later, it was still a case we were Like Poles, with a strangely compelling repulsion that sort of bounced between us.

Hah, she whispered. *We haven't changed.*

We broke apart and she walked indoors, for once not covering her face from the world.

Grrrhhh said my lads, seeing us 'at it' as they would say, and they had their opinions about her.
That's the first time I've seen her face properly
She's an old bag!
She looks like you, Sarge...

The next day she pulled up in her two-seater runabout and hailed me, reverting to the formal with my lot glued to her every move and the possibility of me and her 'Doing It'. They liked me. They wanted earthquakes to happen for me. I think I did, too, but with my sister!? These days, that would be illegal. Sex with sisters can create monsters, as the pharaohs eventually learned.
Would you carry this Mr. Steele?

'This' being a very large piece of exotic wood three foot square and almost two inches thick, engraved with coloured letters and numbers.

I nodded, grabbed it by the edges, hauled it out of the boot and headed toward her rooms where Maxwell was still flat out after the 'medicines' that Beardmore had brought.
It's a planchette.

Of course, she had to call it a 'planchette' to impress The Drip. Being a French word, it sounded so much more impressive than 'Ouija Board'. These were all the rage after the War, when so many lost people tried to contact so many lost souls. You could create your own Ouija with an upturned glass and letters on paper and power it with a shaky hand, so many did.
Are you impressed, Mr. Steele?
I am not, Miss Morgan, not at all.

I thought her grand device rather pitiful. Almost like a prop used by those snake-oil salesmen you read about in the Penny Westerns.
It told me where a secret cave is, within this headland, she whispered, as I carried it into her living room, where I was surprised to see that all the chairs had their legs sawn off and were arranged around the walls.
I'm sure it did, Miss Morgan.

If I removed my boots and socks and stood barefoot on the ground and flicked a certain switch in my mind, then I become a dowsing rod. I think, when people first lived on this ridge before the Bronze Age, most of them had this natural ability. Me, old Silurian that I am, I feel the striations and structures of the land beneath when I go into mode. I feel, become, the cavities and understreams. The gold and the fossils and the bones of creatures now extinct are in my bones. For me, planchettes are little better than the slates my Fleur uses to chalk her letters on ...

I also helped her unpack the costume that she had presumably worn for her appearances in panto: a heavy bluey-black, hooded velvet cloak that was studded with spindly five-rayed silver stars, silver sandals and various silvery head-pieces that – I imagined – would give her moon-like horns.

They spent a lot of time with that planchette. They were children. It seems they had picked up a spiritual guide they called the Priest of the Moon. And said Priest was slowly revealing, letter by letter, word by word, a secret cave below the Fort, within the Down, where mighty magics would be worked. Actually – and I sound a bit like Miss Morgan saying that - but *actually* I knew exactly where it was. On July 6th 1900 a troubled lad called Gunner Haines had fired a ball cartridge down a ventilator shaft right into No. 3 magazine which held 3 tons of gunpowder. The explosion could be heard from Cardiff. He went insane because, I think, he saw things on his lonely night watches that no-one else believed. He told me, a mere lance-corporal, who didn't quite know what to say, or whether I dare reveal myself; and he also told our colonel and the local vicar, but none of us could help him. The thick concrete of the barracks saved my life and the 'thickness' or earthiness of my own Spirit protected me from other things – but only just. I knew the power of the Deep Earth then, that came to me... No-one knows what demons he saw, or whether this was somehow connected with the suicide of our good Captain who was known to be *very* fond of him, but its use as an actual Fort ended then.

As for this 'secret cave' within Brean Down that was apparently obsessing Messrs Maxwell and Morgan, there was still a small, easily missed path off the road that led to the old armoury, but the whole thing had been completely collapsed years ago.

There was something about all this that did not ring true. I have always had my own Two Sights, as Carstairs was the first to notice, though I have no idea where it came from. Apart from seeing the Misty People and Sir Edern and the Fays and the sort of spirits that teemed endlessly across the battlefields of Flanders, it also worked in very odd other ways: I could always tell if one of the 7" shells I was loading my howitzer with was actually a dud. A lot of them were filled in arsenals in America, by German immigrants, so of course they were not as meticulous about loading them as the loyal British women were in Woolwich Arsenal. I can't explain how I knew there was something remiss. Perhaps I could smell that the powder was wrong? Perhaps it was the blood-soaked Land that was protecting me, sending messages upward from my boots and into my hands, via the Mysteries of Touch that Ethel mused about?

And so here at the Fort I had the same feeling during all their work with the Ouija Board. At one point I heard their voices and also a completely different voice joining in. I wondered if another drug dealer had joined them until I read in the Maxwell's *Journal* about that phantom-like 'Priest of the Moon' they had summoned, who never had anything particularly interesting to say.

That might have fooled the drugged-up Maxwell but I knew it was nonsense. In my memory I time-travelled back to the Abaris, sitting next to Vivien again. There she was with the dolly she called Fluff, that she had dressed like a witch with a small broom and tall hat, doing ventriloquism and making it talk. The other children marvelled and believed it was alive. They gave her pennies to make Fluff talk. She earned several shillings that way and never shared. I reproached her for this and many other cons but her invariable reply was always: *You. Are. Jealous.* I always laughed and walked away. She was doing something similar now, here on the Fort, and Maxwell with his child-like soul fell for it too. I'd wager it was costing him more than pennies. I'd also wager that she was vamping other men in the area, which is why she was absent so often.

Over the years, I had read in many newspapers and lurid magazines of people getting excited by the imminent discovery of the Hall of Records underneath the Sphinx that would contain all the knowledge of lost Atlantis. And of caves in the Himalayas that contained records of lost Lemuria. Or Cities of Gold in the Amazon rain-forests. Then again there was also a dozen caves across Britain and France, it seemed, where King Arthur and his Knights lay sleeping, just awaiting discovery from the perfect person. As I said, 'The Father' – Carstairs - felt that they were actually lying in a cave below Brent Knoll, which is why I spent so much time wandering and wondering on its slopes. I heard the Knights whispering, rippling the grasses. They seemed to like me. They insisted:

Serve, Serve, Serve.
Serve what? Serve who?
The Land and its People.

And here, where two kingdoms met, Sir Edern himself appeared, a scrawny little fellow, not at all Knightly, though he did bear an heraldic symbol, a sort of red badge with three lions heads in profile. I never did learn what it meant. But he looked more like Robin Hood than any sort of knight: long black hair, a hooded jerkin and calf-length leather boots. He didn't wear armour (why would he need it?) but his clothes under the glorious cloak of swan feathers were of the Earth – citrine, olive, russet, and black. If he stepped between the trees he would have become invisible unless you knew where to look – or perhaps *How* to look. Plus he held this aura of Worry before him as other Knights might hold a shield. If he was truly the Son of Nudd, the Son of Darkness, then his torment came from sacrifices other than from battling the three giants within the Knoll. He told me:

We are One.

I nodded. I seemed to know him. Who needed a Priest of the Moon when I had this Priest of the Earth? I told him:

I want to know.

Then you must Serve. There is a Great War coming unlike any ever known. You will be needed. You will shake the earth and bring down fire from the heavens.

I knew straight away that meant the Royal Artillery.

Which is why I ran away to join the Army. I needed to be needed.

I think Carstairs knew all about Sir Edern and his connection with Morgan le Fay, and thus with me, and that Swans were going to be very busy in the next few years taking the dead souls of Somerset into the North. He told me that 'Edern' comes from Aeturnus, meaning eternal or immortal. But Mrs Carstairs corrected him (quite sharply in fact) and said it came from the Welsh 'Edyrn', meaning immense, or wonderful. *Edern ap Nudd – remember that Master Steele,* she told me.

And I did.

So... all of this at the Fort with Maxwell and Miss Morgan and their Ouija Board made the small side of me think about all those fortune-tellers, crystal-gazers, tea-cup twisters and a thousand materialising mediums who had people enthralled. That's apart from the tricksters and 'confidence artists' I read about who made fortunes selling London Bridge, the Eiffel Tower and Brooklyn Bridge to gullible tourists with more money than sense. Perhaps I am being unfair suggesting that 'Miss Morgan' was selling impossible things. She had to make a living somehow and so did I, as a builder or carpenter. But I have often wondered about that Russian woman, Madame Blavatsky, passing on hand-written messages that she insisted came from Himalayan 'Masters'. Messages that had no spiritual value that I could see.

Could people like that be 'phoneys', as the American doughboys who came over with General Pershing might have said?[9]

But also...

The real thing at the same time?

I might have asked Carstairs if he had still been around, though he probably would have made a joke or come out with some nonsense about the Way of the Fool and how everything that can happen does happen - which should have been the School Motto, if you ask me.

There came that priceless moment when they lit this *Fire of Azrael* thing...

At the very tip of the rocks, just beyond that 'Frenulum' of hers, there was a flat, table-like surface of rock that had been built to enable delivery of supplies from local boats at lowest tide. She was in her gown of sea-green silk, he had his trousers rolled up his scrawny legs and was in his shirt-sleeves, with a devil-may-care slightly-loosened tie. They were building a pyramid of boughs – juniper I think – that were then scattered with cedar and sandalwood bits and pieces. I wondered if the packets of heroin he had picked up from the Tibetan in Bristol were being disposed of in case of a police raid. The wine-waiter at *The George* had recently been arrested, but it was more likely to be for

---

[9] 'Black Jack' Pershing was commander of the American Expeditionary Forces from 1917-1920.

'unnatural acts' than dealing drugs, about which the local Bobbies were all too ignorant.

I don't think Maxwell had ever worked so hard. There were a few crab-catchers in the bay who looked in their direction but it seemed that The Drip was under strict orders, like that woman in the Underworld, not to look around but keep to the task in hand, racing against time and tide. Then when the tide did begin to turn he put matches to the pile. Of course, he couldn't get it to light. He had probably never lit a real fire in his easy life, never did more than say to a servant: *Do something about that fire, would you?* Thin, pitiful salamanders of smoke rose from the pile that was named after Azrael the Angel of Death. If they sought immortality that way, then it was the wrong sort of magic.

Me and the lads had paused for a tea break and were watching all this from the front yard. I could feel his exasperation flowing down his puny stick-like legs and slithering across the rocks, racing against the rising pulses of waters.

Miss Morgan turned and looked at me. I knew exactly what she wanted. It took but a moment for me to remove the can of petrol from the back of her run-about and hand it to him out at the rock, taking care that my big heavy boots didn't step on his noble, bare feet. He took it without thanking me. But she did, silently, a smile in her strange eyes. I went back to the Fort, knowing he was as likely to burn himself as the pyre.

He soaked the pile with petrol, applied the match. He assumed it would be like paraffin (a gentle *foomf* as it took alight) and never understood what happened within the engine of his car, or anything about internal combustion. Of course it exploded, as petrol does, knocking them both off their feet but at least igniting the woods whether the woods themselves wanted igniting or not. Flames leapt from twig to twig, smoke and fumes and a number of real salamanders rose like genies and enveloped them. He was horrified. I could see that Miss Morgan was enjoying every moment, coughing with delight. (She once started a small fire in the small gym at our small school, although *I* got the blame. Carstairs just laughed and came out with some annoying philosophy and we all had a small party there - after I had been made to repaint the walls. When the cakes came around someone asked: *Where is Vivien?* But she was gone.)

Then the first ripple of the sea washed over the level rock and met the burning base and we could hear the serpent-hissing from the sea-walls.

Tom was bemused:
What was the point of that?
Dick was bemused:
Nutters.
Harry:
He'd do anything for a bit of you-know-what, wouldn't he sarge?
I expect he would. Wouldn't you? Now lads, lets fix that last bit of roof. But spin it out. It's their money going up in smoke.

I can't say that their Priest of Moon was *all* smoke and mirrors. Otherwise what did that make Sir Edern and all the multitude of Beings that have risen to me from the Inner Earth? It bothers me to consider this. There is no doubt that 'Vivien le Fay Morgan', as she styled herself, was able to connect with strange forces. But I would never admit this to the girl I had once known as 'Viv'. I suppose it was like adjusting the dials of one of those 'wireless' devices that Marconi had developed (here in the Fort, actually, shortly after my time!) sending experimental but flowing energies across to Barry Island. Perhaps that is what 'Miss Morgan' herself actually was: an electric impulse, full of invisible waves. Perhaps that is what we all are.

As for that third voice I overheard when they were at it in their little Temple – for that is what it was – even *that* could have been genuine. I had had a little experience of the 'Direct Voice' mediumship that many were demonstrating in those years - not always honestly. I am also willing to 'stand down', as old soldiers eventually must, and consider that it may have been my *own* inner senses that heard this, as none of my lads turned a hair. Once, on leave in London, immediately after a Zeppelin bombed a school I was passing, I heard a Direct Voice from someone or something calling himself 'Mickey'.

Look under that wall, quickly! it said.

I was young, strong, this was my element. I heaved the bricks aside and from the cloud of grey, choking dust pulled out a very scared and battered and also very lucky young boy.

What's your name, laddy? I asked gently, holding him to stop the shakes I understood only too well.

Leslie... Leslie Flint he gasped.

Flint by name and Flint by nature I said, impressed by his earthy-hardness, though that was lost on him. Years later I learned that he became something of star in the world of Direct Voice mediumship and claimed he owed it all to this 'Mickey'.[10]

Perhaps there *was* something genuine of that nature occurring within the Fort. As long as me and the lads got paid I could hardly interfere.

Maxwell went into coherent detail in his *Secret Journal* that I, Scottie and Ethel devoured like it was the scandalous Daily Mail. He said a lot of hurtful things about his sister and actually boasted about slapping her. He wrote: *Ethel knows as much about cooking as I do about ballooning and cared no more. She considers herself a good housewife on the strength of seeing to it that the lace curtains were clean and the steps kept white.*

What a bitch, hissed Ethel when she read this and then: *Cochon!*

Mais non, un espèce de merde.

I was pleased to see she her startled by my grasp of French.

You are a man of depth, Daniel.

Depth, height, length and breadth...

From Saint Bernard?

The dog?

You tease. Bernard of Clairvaux! That was his definition of God.

Was he in the artillery?

You're definitely teasing.

Do you mind?

No.

There are holes in your soul Daniel.

Shrapnel...

She smiled and turned her attention back to the Journal, turning the pages with her index finger and thumb at the top corner, as if they were infected. I could sense a shift of mood, another lightening toward me. I think she knew, even then, that I would smash and bash Maxwell if he ever struck her (or anyone!) in my presence. He also described Fleur as

---

[10] Leslie Flint, 1911-94, whose familiar 'Mickey' saved him exactly as Steele describes here.

a 'parody of humanity', which was cruel, downright wrong, and totally unnecessary, but at least proved what a piece of shit he really was.

Yet he tried to describe their Priest of the Moon in coherent, none-doped prose that was always written in red ink. So I suppose his motives were not too different to those of Madame Blavatsky when she got the words of the Mahatmas into the head of A.P. Sinnet and eventually the entire and disbelieving world.

There was an awful lot about Persephone, the Queen of Hades, Aphrodite and Dark Queens that meant nothing to me. And more stuff about tides of flux and reflux and souls of men ebbing and flowing. It seemed to me that if the Priest of the Moon had ever been incarnate, then he had never been to sea with real, hard-working fishermen because they would have thrown him overboard after an hour of his pompous comments. At one point, heavily underlined, the Priest of the Moon reproached Maxwell for the wretch he knew himself to be: *Why fear ye the Dark Queen?* he demanded of The Drip. And there was a long piece in which that Being lectured about the 'two deaths' by which men die: the Death of the Body and the Death of Initiation, and of course the latter was greater.

So *he* said.

I didn't need to be a Master of Graphology to see Maxwell's guilt and shame screaming silently about him never having served in the War. Nor ever having done anything useful or brave or manly in his sad, shallow, wet, pointless little life. Once he achieved his 'initiation' via his Sea Priestess then the Priest of the Moon promised him that he could go by 'the path of the well-head that is beside the white cypress' - whatever that meant.

I imagined it was some place out by the woods at Kewstoke.

There was also his obsession with the Atlantean upbringing of the 'Sea Priestess'. Again and again he transcribed her tales of having been raised in a secluded Sun Temple, knowing nothing of males and the male world when growing up and how, silently and secretly, chosen females were removed by priests from their dormitories in the middle of the night to be mated with exalted Adepts of some Sacred Clan. 'It was an ordered rite' he wrote, and that made my nape hairs prickle: 'corresponding to processes in Great Nature herself.'

It sounded like the *droit du seigneur* that allowed the Lords of Somerset to take the virginity of any female on demand. Ethel touched my hand. I shuddered.

Your brother is a sick man.

He always was. He took after our pater – the Unknown Master we called him, as we saw so little of him.

'Morgan the Sea Borne' might have arrived at Brent Knoll from a place now known as South Wales, but I suppose she might have carried within herself histories and impulses so ancient that she really had come from the City of Golden Gates in lost Atlantis.

As I say that I had an instant memory of that Captain who killed himself at the Fort. (A memory or a ghost? Is there a difference?) I say this because when he was not in uniform he always wore a tie. Almost all men did in those days, but *his* tie sent out histories and pulses of a similar kind. It bore light-blue diagonal stripes on a black background and proclaimed to the entire world that he had gone to Eton, and was thus *crème de la crème*. The Captain was tied to Eton; Vivien to Atlantis. I think we can *all* carry ancient atmospheres within us, sending them out like the searchlight that once rayed out from the tip of the Fort.

There was a morning of thin blue sky over the Fort, a high tide and clusters of seagulls skrawking around and above the trawlers. I was reminded of the shrapnel bursts I could summon from my trusty Quick-Fire Field Howitzer – 500 metal balls that would explode fifty feet above the German wire and make it passable for the Tommies.

To the east there was something going on in the bay near the Woodspring Priory, a sad haunted place that had something to do with one of the knights who murdered Thomas Becket. Carstairs gave us all a long talk about this once but I'd withdrawn my thoughts like the tide and daydreamed about joining the Army instead. While to the south the nine-legged Burnham lighthouse presided over its sands like an underworld beast. Carstairs once told us a story about some god who had a nine-legged steed, and I always supposed this might have been the inspiration for the architect.

You're thinking of Odin's horse, Sleipnir, whispered Miss Morgan from behind me. With the noise of the gulls I didn't hear her approach. Then again, after years of cannon fire, my hearing is not *quite* as good as it used to be.

You still read thoughts, I whispered back, without turning.

Sometimes. And the horse had eight legs, not nine.

Does that matter?

It did to the horse. Now then, - actually – I want you to create some Moon Pyramids.

Maxwell had come out to join us. He was in a double-breasted suit with skewed bow-tie and tilted fedora. Men of his class couldn't be seen outside bare-headed could they? He stood swaying next to her, nodding vacantly, the dope behind his eyes like fog in the Channel.

Moon Pyramids? I wondered if she was having some memory of a past life. At that time some chap called Howard Carter was opening a tomb in Egypt that everyone was excited about. Depending on their station in life there were suddenly masses of folk remembering that they had been High Priests or High Priestesses and not a few (usually with double-barrelled names) who had been actual Pharaohs. It seemed that you weren't anyone unless you had at least one incarnation in Egypt. I had actually spent some time there with my regiment but I can't say anything reached up through the layers of burning sand, camel dung and Mohammedism.

Then again, a lot of the gentry here in England spent their private fortunes ripping open the local mounds and barrows that predated Stonehenge in the hope of similar glory and gold. They never found much either, as far as I understood. I never read the quality journals that might tell me otherwise. As a lad I used to daydream about taking a team and digging deep into Brent Knoll to find the Sleeping Knights that the Carstairs told me about. I suppose I'm not too different to Miss Morgan and the 'secret cave' she tempts Maxwell with here within Brean Down, although I see that as some kind of sexual thing. Or have I been reading too much about this 'Psychology' in that book we found? The more I see and overhear about their relationship the more I think she was just being a prick-teaser.

What 'moon pyramids would those be, Miss Morgan?

She made a vague gesture toward the upper slopes of the hill then snapped at her companion:

Go and lie down Wilfred, you're over-tired. I'll deal with Mr. Steele.

The term 'whipped cur' floated into my mind like a piece of jetsam - and clearly into those of my lads too. They were loving it, seeing what the posh folk were really like. They couldn't get over seeing him applying paint in sticky streaks to one of his murals, using his own hair comb.

He's obsessed with those scattered cairns that run along the spine of the Down. They remind him of something Atlantean.

I hadn't noticed them. She read my thoughts again, from my frown. Apparently, twins often have telepathic powers.

Lots of white stones. A processional way. They used to be cairns, two by two, but got scattered. He wants them rebuilt as pyramids. Five feet high.

I said nothing. I *had* seen the stones. Assumed they were left over from an attempt at an access road when they built the Fort.

Why is this important?
He thinks they were created by a forgotten college of priests.
*Do **you** think that?*
She smiled.
Wilfred does like the idea of priests and warriors.
Why not a forgotten college of nuns or nurses?
He's never really left that boarding school of his, has he?
His sort never does.

She knew exactly what I meant by 'his sort'.

Apparently, the rebuilding work you did with the broken-down drystone walls of Mr. Chichester is widely admired in town. Wilfred wants you to do the same here, making small pyramids instead of walls.

More money for me and the lads.
Is that all you care about?
In this day and age, yes. I don't care what silly game you're playing.
*Dan Danny Danieeeel... You're still eaten up with jealousy aren't you? But what if it's **not** a silly game?*

I shrugged and started off up the hill. Across the waters behind us, above the dark mountains on the other side of the Channel, storm clouds were gathering across Wales. They would reach us soon.

It took us a little while to walk up the narrow spine of the land. The grass here was slippery with dew but the Bluebells were out on the lower slopes at either side. Every Spring at this time people walked or bicycled here from Weston or Burnham just to absorb them. I say 'absorb' because that's what I feel. For me, they seem to radiate innocence and purity and wishful times. I put my open palms above them and feel their soft energies rising, like a breeze. A sort of gentle electricity. Some old soldiers tell me they get the same from poppies, but then again, they'd never experienced this curving Milky Way of Poppies on Brean Down.

Viv kept slipping on the grass, oblivious to the Bluebell road in my own secret sky. She tried to take my hand or arm for support but I kept slightly ahead.

Pig she snorted. *Actually,* **Jealous** *Pig. You know it's true.*

I said nothing. I was afraid of her touch. It was the Twin Thing. The Magnet Thing. I doubt if there was anything about these in that thin, grim book called 'Psychology'. And I also didn't want the History Thing in which our conversation might open like one of Carstairs old school books: not so much 'Peter Parley's Tales of Greece and Rome' that every school had, but the as yet unwritten 'Tales of Lost Atlantis' that she was injecting Maxwell with.

The white stones, she panted. *See…*

I did see. White limestone, soft and carve-able. Not local. I've found this stone can also heal and purify.

You carved me a little figurine at school, remember?

I did.

No, I lied, but I remember it had been a fat little goddess.

It was a fat little goddess, Danny. I called her Danuih.

I looked at these scattered stones with a new eye. When I'd first seen them, half a lifetime ago, I thought they were just the messily discarded remnants of something the Army had started, some road or building. Now, with Viv having put the words into my mind, I saw the 'Moon Pyramids' spring up and form a shining avenue along the spine.

Ah! she said, sharp as a needle. *You* **do** *remember. The old Festival of Air in the Old Country, and the worship of our ancestor Ta-Khu. This is from* **Atlantis**, *Daniel, everything always comes back to* **Atlantis** *for homeless souls like us.*

Air Festival? Ta-Khu? The odd name sounded oddly familiar. Ta-Khu... Ta-Khu...

Viv stood in front of me, hands on my temples.

*Danny, remember also the Fire Festival invoking the goddesses Khiet-Sin and Philaeia. Then the Water Festival with the dancing and singing for the mighty Khe-Ta. And never forgetting your own Earth Festival that was also known as the 'The Time of the Children', to round it all off. That was when you, personally, invoked and made manifest the Akhantuih and the Danuih. That's how you got your name. Dan Daniel Danny **Danuih**. Remember, wake up!*

I was troubled, I don't deny it. There was a storm manifesting from the bitter seas of the Channel and something similar in my own mind: Such strange names that weren't strange at all. I was back in the school room at Abaris and trying to absorb what The Father was telling me. Ta-Khu. Khiet-Sin. Khe-Ta. Danuih. Akhantuih. The latter was a wolf-like energy that seemed to loom and smile at me.[11]

Vivien nudged me. She seemed amused.

These things will all be remembered, renewed and made good here in the West Country.

These things?

Atlantean things you dummy. For starters, Wilfred wants a processional way of small pyramids, two by two, ending at two upright stones with a lintel, like Stonehenge.

Perhaps Wilfred Maxwell with his dreams of these 'Moon Pyramids' knew more than I was willing to admit. Or perhaps Miss Morgan had injected me with her visions just as sharply as Beardmore's needle did with his dope. Still, I saw them clearly and wondered whether white Caen Stone might be nobler and more powerful than quartz, and if Maxwell could or would afford it. At that moment, under glowering skies both within and without, I only needed to use one ritual movement and say one Word of Power to regain my balance.

I moved my left foot and brought my heels together at a 45-degree angle, bringing my spine to align with my right foot. A lot of people never understand that *only* the left foot can shift to get into the proper stance. A lot of people never get to utter the single Word that could paralyse a whole Army when uttered by the appropriate God – usually a Regimental Colonel.

---

[11] These beings were also channelled by the deva Murry Hope (1929-2012)

ATTEN-***SHUN!***

It felt good to utter, believe me. Then I blinked. Three times, slowly, like an owl. 'Back to earth, Daniel', I whispered to myself, stamping my big boots on the ground and standing to attention in my soldierly way. The nonsense names and their visions scattered like mice. I could smell her perfume, the usual camphor, not at all sensual.

*You can't hypnotise **me**, 'Miss Morgan'.*

I would never try.

You're using him.

Stuff and nonsense! And I do wish you'd call me Viv. Or even Sis.

***Viv**. We'll build what he wants if he pays up front.*

He will pay. I will make sure of that.

*You're using him. **Viv**.*

There...that wasn't so hard, Danny was it? Actually... so are you.

I shrugged.

I'm no fool, dear brother of mine. You're all working slowly, ridiculously so, stringing the work out.

Can you blame us?

*Not at all. Dan, Danny, Danuih, **Daniel** dear... As well as this cancerous jealousy, I know you're afraid of me. Most men are. Actually, what I really think is –*

I cut her off.

Listen!

I could hear something odd, sliding under the calling of crows. A sort of rhythmic, repetitive chanting as the daytime wind from the land to sea carried it up to us in little wavelets of sound.

*Io Pan, Io Pan, Io Pan Pan **Pan**... Io Pan, Io Pan, Io Pan Pan **Pan**...*

A man and woman, younger than us, panted hand-in-hand up the steep slopes. Or she did, as the man looked in good shape. Although I hadn't seen him for a few years I knew him at once: dark haired, powerful in build, neatly suited and booted as though he might now have some profession other than soldiering.

The woman was what might be called 'sensibly dressed' with tweed coat, calf-length dress and 'sensible' shoes that might be good in Town, but not ideal for the top of Brean Down. She had long strawberry-blonde hair that was kinked, as though she normally kept it bound. I felt she was older, and they were – somehow - both slightly embarrassed with each other.

Odd couple, I thought.

Odd couple, said Viv.

They looked startled when they saw us, the man actually blushed. He was blinking into the sun and didn't recognise my ugly mush at first. Plus my hair was longer and I was growing a slight beard.

It's not often we hear Pan invoked in Somersetshire, I offered, to make him feel at ease.

He shrugged, said nothing because the woman elbowed him, but he looked at me and then it clicked: the two Old Soldiers inside us began communing. They always recognise kindred souls, Old Soldiers do. Perhaps it is just the bearing, or the worry lines. This man clearly carried a tumbling cloud of war-remembrance. Yet he still looked as if he could handle himself. His eyes fastened on the Artillery cap-badge I always wore like a medal and his words exploded like a Stoke's Mortar.

*Violet, this.... **this** is Sergeant Steele! Sergeant. **Steele**!*

Those words in their rich Welsh accent summoned up all sorts of ghosts.

Mr. *Steele these days, Penry.*

He pointed to the badge and explained to the women: *He was in the Royal Artillery and I was in the Suicide Squad.*

Also known as the Machine Gun Corps, I explained.

That's right. Machine Gun Corps of the Artists Rifles. He was my instructor at Rolleston Camp, Vi. I was transferred there as a mere lance-corporal. Remember?

How could I forget? I retained his name like a piece of shrapnel that never quite wiggles its way out. I worked with a lot of men in those days, living and dead. There were numberless ghouls on The Plain - shades that floated there before Stonehenge was built and will be there when it's long forgotten. But this very human chap had stayed in my mind and I stumbled on his progress after the War in local newspapers. From absolute nothingness 'Merl', as he was nicknamed, seemed to be doing quite well for himself.

Sarge taught me everything! All about cones of fire and trajectory of machine-gun bullets and how to use the ruler and protractor to determine position. You saved me from jankers when you slyly helped me adjust that rusty clinometer on my Vickers. Remember?

The new camp was like one of those assembly lines that Henry Ford boasted about, but I did remember him, even though I'd taught so many others. Deep calling to Deep, or Fire to Fire, perhaps.

Dear old Machine Gun Corps...You know they've just been disbanded?

Who would need us now, after our War to end all Wars, eh Sarge?

For a second, we were both back there on the bleak Plain within shooting distance of Stonehenge itself. Machine Gunners in those days were a new breed, a form of artillery that no-one knew exactly how to use. I was tasked with teaching them my own artillery science: shell-weight, powder-weight, gravity and air pressures; rifled and smooth bore barrels and arcs of fire; windspeed, elevation, humidity and especially the rotation of the Earth and the angles of its Sun. All so that we could pour fire down on the Huns skulking unseen far behind their own front lines, hoping that our hot lead would transform into the gold of Victory.

Yet they got a bad deal, the machine gunners. Unlike riflemen, with single shots directly at an observable target, the gunners had to rake the air above and beyond the immediate enemy lines. It could seem to the ordinary Tommy that these Vickers machine-guns were firing useless arcs into the air, and that their gunners were effectively hiding. Artillery men like me were often accused of the same thing for using the same techniques; yet we destroyed the unsee-able enemy beyond the far horizon. If our lines were ever over-run by the Huns, no mercy was ever given to the likes of him or us. Hence the nickname 'Suicide Squad'.

I could sense our female companions were irritated by our instant commune; they were sizing each other up as I think women sometimes do, though I can't say I've known enough of them to be sure. The man's companion couldn't take her eyes off Viv, who, with her flowing gown, heavy make-up, vivid lipstick and wild, heavily-dyed black hair being ruffled by the increasing wind, must have appeared on that hill-top like a Witch Queen from a pantomime.

Are you lost? asked Viv with a tone that clearly meant 'Go Away'. What did she care about a strange Welshman invoking Pan?

The woman shook her head. There was an awkwardness that I found amusing. It was almost as though they were having a staring contest, or trying to hypnotise each other. I could see the man was amused too, and that clearly irritated both. The air between them quivered. If you had dropped a crow's feather into the maelstrom it would have spiralled upward. If Old Soldiers can share minds, perhaps these two women were doing similar.

I don't know about Viv but I was getting that 'continuation' thing again - though that might not be the right word. I'm better describing the use of high explosive shells than explosive things within our thoughts.

Have you ever met someone and felt Silence descend and have the feeling you're in a bell jar? That is not *exactly* what I mean. This is not 'love at first sight', or anything to do with 'past lives' that people use to justify extra-marital affairs and bad behaviour generally. It's a sense that you are somehow connected to this stranger whom you are never likely to see again. There is no need to say anything; you are joined by the stillness and a feeling of being beyond Time. Then – *actually!* - you both carry on carrying on and never see each other again.

I was feeling the world and its Time stopping now quite intensely, as it never quite did with Penry during the War when Duty, Flanders, France and the water-cooled .303 Vickers Gun called.

I like to imagine that at some time, tens of thousands of years ago in a forgotten realm far to the West, some wild hunter mated with a woman who had something special in her blood that was passed on to her offspring, spiralling down the endless rivulets of Time and resulting in me and this man who had just emerged from the Bluebells, carrying a kinship of Silence. If I'd been a Theosophist I'd probably talk about reincarnation and create all sorts of stories, like Mrs Besant and that decidedly odd Reverend Leadbeater seem to do. But I think this is something else within that is deeper; something below and beyond and within the blood, perhaps. I suppose I've got Hidden Cave within me after all. Maybe 'Vivien le Fay Morgan', whatever or whoever she might be, might help me find it.

Jolly nice to meet you both! said this Violet with a forced and lying smile. *We're **actually** heading toward Brent Knoll but the bluebells of this hill called us first. Do you know the Knoll?*

Had *she* seen the pictures in my mind also? Was I that transparent?

Actually...Actually...Actually... I felt that this odd couple was a continuation of me and Viv. They lived within us, and we them, and that's another thing not easy to explain.

The man was Welsh and I just *knew* that the woman was too, despite her English accent. In my own orphan daydreams, I like to imagine that my parents came from the deepest darkest depths of the lost continent with strange gods and forgotten tongues that became known as Wales. For the instant it took for this approaching couple to take a single step, I was back at school on the Knoll with Viv telling me that we were of those pre-Keltic people from the central mountain mass of mid-Wales. She told me, whispering, that *actually* these people were Atlantean, drawn to these islands by trade and then surviving when the catastrophe happened. She said at the time: *Daniel, this is why we feel different. This is why we have a remoteness of soul. We. Do. Not. Fully. Belong.*

I saw it all happen, Ages in an Instant. I had to blink, blink blink. I think Violet might have glimpsed the story-lines and the histories within me. Within us.

And hence the four of us stood together on that hilltop, four tuning forks quivering to each other's notes. Daniel and Vivien; Penry and Violet. Were we, somehow, quadruplets!?

Then I stepped forward and pointed toward the Knoll. It rose as a perfect pyramid from the wide waste of the marshes. Fir trees clustered in the folds of its sides but the crest of it was bare to the winds.

See? I asked Penry, and I think he did. I think he 'saw' where the Oldest Worship was held, not here on the Down. I found myself almost shoulder to shoulder with him, forming a line as Old Soldiers naturally do. It did seem to catch a loose burst of sunlight and almost glow. I wasn't sure if this came from the sky above or the geologies below, welcoming the attention.

At least it's not Hill 60, he whispered. I felt waves of his sorrow at the memory of that fell place, and the death, and the mud, and the warriors of a far country and the utterly senseless sacrifice – for what? Some inbred King and his foreign Queen?

There are some things that can never be explained.

An old fella in town told me you were up here, Sarge. You made a mess of his wall, he said you were a cowboy.

What did old Chichester know about anything? I was more concerned that the stone-grey sea-mist in the Channel was advancing toward us like the massed Fritzies felt they had to do, in the last year of the War, when they knew they were losing - thanks to me and my weaponry. And Penry with his machine guns. Yet I wondered if this turbulence was being summoned by The Violet or The Vivien, as I suddenly thought of them. Or maybe even Merl himself! Old Soldiers like him (and me) can often attract such energies whether we mean to or not. The Magnet Thing again, I suppose.

The land before the Knoll used to be under a shallow sea, said The Vivien, doing the polite. *Traders came from across the known and unknown worlds.*

In your time? asked The Violet.

Actually, thousands and thousands and **thousands** *of years ago.*

The four of us now stood bunched, a round unit, and I thought of that big crystal ball I'd read about in Maxwell's Secret Diary. We were enfolded, somehow, in a universe that was interconnected. I'm sure we all saw, and became, those people that Maxwell had written about in such lurid terms: the processional way to the temple on the crest of the mist-crowned sacred mountain, the men in high-prowed boats, the shaven priests and bearded warriors, the holy trade of deep-earth substances involving tin; the great chambers of the caves beneath where secret worship was held and the endless contending of land and sea and even the curious grey seals that might have been mermaids.

The Vivien broke the silence, trying to make some point:

We went to the **Abaris** *School there, Danny and I. You can probably just see it, see the light from the little tower? Our master was Mr.* **Carstairs.** *You'll have heard of him no doubt.*

Did Penry guess that the Special School on Brent Knoll was also a sort of Sacred College on 'Bell Knowle'?

Violet blinked, then looked oddly vacant. Perhaps she saw both. I'd seen that look before in epileptics, before their grand mal. I knew a man who did this in the trenches, to get sent back down the line.

Vi...Vi...Violet said Penry, who also recognised the onset of either a petit or a grand mal.

Violet emerged as if from that ball of spinning, revolving thoughts. We surrounded her with silence. Then…she shook her head, her eyes cleared. She came back to us.

Penry looked at me and gave shrug. No big deal. The Vivien swallowed hard and then:

I'd heard about your senior master Carstairs. I used to go to a rival boarding school just down the road in Bruton. Sexey's School of Excellence. It cost a fortune to send me there. God knows a fortune.

*We certainly heard of **that** place didn't we Daniel?* as though there were dirty secrets attached.

We did, but there was nothing much to hear, no more than a leaf falling from a tree. Nothing that I was aware of. Yet that comment seemed to touch a nerve: Violet's response was sharp.

*And we all heard of **your** place too!*

Then the storm hit us.

Time to go, we heard ourselves saying in unison as we bowed to the power of the sylphs and undines.

Hope you liked our Bluebells… said The Vivien directly to Penry. I think she was flirting. He smiled.

I prefer Welsh Daffodils myself. Hwyl am y tro![12]

The Violet punched him on the arm as they bent into the rain and headed off back down the hill, her slipping and tripping.

Penry handed me a simple address card.

If you're ever in London…

She punched his arm again.

I don't she likes him being Welsh, I thought.

I don't think she likes him being working class, said Viv.

Then came the Days and Nights of The Storm. I wondered if the things that Maxwell and Miss Morgan were doing up at the Fort had triggered this. I know that when Marconi[13] was sending his electric waves across the waters, a few years earlier, many locals feared he would interfere with the weather. I doubt if anyone kept records to prove this but the fisherfolk themselves blamed him for the unexpected furies of the elements. The deep waters in the Bristol Channel had the highest tides

---
[12] Goodbye for now.

[13] 1874-1937. Italian inventor of 'wireless telegraphy' that became known as radio.

in the British Isles and the currents could be irrational, implacable and downright murderous[14]. When the fisher folk were doing their 'Channelling', as they sometimes called their work, they needed all the calm they could get. I suppose that if Miss Morgan went into full Sea Priestess mode it is quite likely to have had some local knock-on effects in terms of Water and Air.

Have *I* ever triggered similar perturbations of Earth and Fire? I think so, but that's another story. Besides, at the height of my own powers I was ripping the world apart along the Western Front. Does that count?

I was pleased to have an explosion of extreme weather that was as unforeseen and devastating as the moment when Gunner Haines had fired his gun into the No. 3 magazine.

Or maybe I had foreseen it. Carstairs often said I had that Curse of the Two Sights. I sometimes *knew* of things without knowing that I knew them. When I had agreed to work on the Fort I insisted on a contract. I don't know why. In fact, I assumed that Maxwell would laugh at my cheek but 'Miss Morgan' sort of leaned against him in all sorts of ways and he quickly rattled one off. As detailed in this contract we were still to be paid daily, even if we had days of storm. Maxwell was doped-up and stupid when he scrawled his name on the agreement. Scottie, who signed as a witness to make it entirely legal, whispered to me later:

He could have been signing his soul to the Devil.
Perhaps he did.
You're not the Devil, are you?
Oh how we laughed...

When the hard rain hit the shore and water hurtled down in spears and the thunder blasted like my 9.2-inch howitzers and trees were ripped up in the wind, I gave the lads the day off and left my erstwhile employers in the Fort to their own devices. We had worked hard at making the main buildings as weather-proof as they had ever been and could do no more.

Instead, I took Fleur around to see Ethel as usual. And despite their own fears of thunder and lightning, this turned into one of the best days I'd had in a very long time. They were terrified of the thunder; I put

---

[14] The tidal range on the Severn can be as much as 50ft. The funnel-shaped estuary, causes the incoming tide to form a great 'bore', from beyond Gloucester and roaring back to Brean Down, with rideable waves of 25 miles. It is affected by the Moon.

arms around them both. To me, as an Artillery man, it was merely the world chuckling.

The three of us had a quite a time playing Happy Families. I don't mean metaphorically, I mean the actual card game that Fleur loved, being pitched at the level of 'normal' three-year olds and so just right for her, given her difficulties. We had fun with *Bones, the Butcher, Chip the Carpenter* (whom Ethel assured me was a dead ringer for me*), Dose the Doctor* (who had an uncanny similarity to Beardmore), *Soot the Sweep, Tape the Tailor, Mrs Puts the Painters Wife* and a dozen other characters who bore marked similarities to known worthies of Weston-super-Mare.

Or so we fancied!

Ethel made a great fuss of doing Fleur's hair and told a great lie about some clothes she had found in the loft that she said were as old as the *Happy Families* deck of cards, though they looked very new to my unpractised eye. Strangely enough they just happened to fit Fleur perfectly and made her very fairy-like with all sorts of frills and bright colours. She glowed. They both did. Like the coals in the fire.

Happy Families…I had forgotten how to play the real-life version of that game.

In fact, that is an outright lie – I had *never* known how to do that.

I recall that Wilfred Maxwell began his 'Secret Journal' by pleading guilty to the vice of keeping a detailed account of his life from the earliest of days onward. I will not do that about my wife – Fleur's mother – yet I must acknowledge her.

I met Astrid in France. Her ancestors had been nobles from Brittany and she was a schoolmistress near Amiens. I was to obliterate large areas around that town during the Big Push of August 1918 that finally won us the War. She was on neutral ground when I met her and safe from the actual carnage. We were both in our mid-30s then, and seen as 'old' in the eyes of our peers. She spoke English well and I knew adequate French, having spent two months with the famed *Régiment de la Fère* to share knowledge and master their excellent equipment and also – I must admit – frequent their excellent brothels, all of which were more elegant than those offered to us rough Tommies. Most of the French men who might otherwise have courted Astrid in another world and other days, had been dispatched to the 'meat-grinder' known as Verdun, where nearly a million young *poilus* died in less than a year.

I often hear a questioning voice in my head. It has the brisk, singular tone of our General Haig[15] who, after the slow start at the Somme, came to win us all the battles, so it must come from somewhere near God.

*Sergeant Steele …**Did** you love her?*
She was kind.
*Sergeant Steele … Did you **love** her?*
She seemed to care for me.
*Sergeant Steele!! Did. You. Love. **Her**?*

Alas… I think not Sir.

But I was kind and caring to her in return, as far as any soldier could be whose job is mass slaughter, and we both loved our strange little changeling child. Many local churches in Somersetshire had little carvings on their outer walls representing what they called 'hunkypunks' – will o' the wisps and faeries and sometimes, sadly, the spirits of unbaptised children. We never had Fleur baptised, though I sometimes felt I was being cowardly or else too honest to have this done.

---

[15] Douglas Haig, 1861-1928. Commander of the British Expeditionary Force.

Did Astrid love me? Perhaps not. Yet we got along, though never once used the 'tu' when speaking. I sense her presence sometimes and I think Fleur does too.

So there I was, with Ethel and Fleur, safe within the storm as the thunder rattled the roof and the wind made the noise of banshees at our windows and sailors must have screamed for their mothers or prayed to their neglected God while their small ships sank beneath them in the nearby waters…

Thank you, Ethel. You spoil her.

She needs spoiling.

Your brother calls her an Idiot.

*What does he know about **anything**? Technically, the correct medical term for her condition is 'Mongol'.*

Research into this had been done in France. Astrid knew all about it. I think it ran in her family, but she had been determined not to be ashamed. They used to say it was a lower-class affliction caused by criminality, alcoholism and ignorant parents. Yet it was widely rumoured that Queen Victoria had secret cousins who were cared for in an asylum, and some of the pupils in our school were of that stock. Mongols, that is. They could as easily have been called Tibetans, then the Theosophists would have been bowing all over them.

The fire needed stoking. Before I could, a blast of wind blew smoke down the chimney that swirled into the room like a grey and troublesome djinn and made us both cough and laugh.

I picked out some lumps of coal from the scuttle and placed them on the fire. I could see from the way Ethel looked that she, like her brother, had always told the servants to do this.

Fine load of Somerset Coal, this, Ethel.

And you would know?

After the War, returning to this Land fit for Heroes that Lloyd George promised, it was the only place an old soldier like me could find work. I spent some years underground as a foreman for Frank and Louis Beauchamps' goldmines.

They are my mother's cousins. My mother is a Beauchamp, from Ireland. But why 'goldmines'?

Because they were so productive. There was a big seam stretching from Bishop Sutton to beyond Temple Cloud. I expect I scratched and dug and scuttled hundreds of feet below you without you ever knowing.

Then you know your coal.

I know Somerset coal like others know flowers: Garden Course Coal, Great Course Coal, Firestone Coal, Little Course Coal, Dungy Drift Coal, Coking Coal...

Stop stop stop! she laughed, touching my bare fore-arm, but not removing her hand when my spiel had finished.

The room was still, the storm had stopped. Fleur had curled herself up on the big rug and was having her afternoon nap. I spread a double sheet of an old Times newspaper and held it over the grate to make the flames draw. The paper sucked in and sealed itself on the edges of the fireplace.

You've never seen that before, have you?

No I haven't. There are many things I haven't seen, or done...

Something might have happened then if Scottie hadn't knocked.

Yes? we both said, breaking apart. He poked his excited 'Yorkshire Terrier' face around the door.

Come see the latest guff in his lordships No'-So-Secret Diary...

I peeled the newspaper off and threw it into the roaring flames. Then I hefted put the brass fireguard in place while Ethel tucked Fleur's special blanket around so that she looked like seal. She'd been a little 'chesty' lately and that was something you had to watch out for in Mongols, as many of them died from chest infections. We left her there, snoring into her dreams, twitching slightly and chasing rabbits down their holes.

What's my lunatic brother saying now?

Scottie made sure that the outer door to Wilfred's office was locked and no servants were around to peer through keyholes, then jabbed at the latest entry with the accusing finger of a priest. I read out the new lines where he asked himself...

Was Miss Morgan a fraud all along?
YES! we said in unison.
Was she sincere but self-deluded?
NO! we said in unison
Was she right in her faith and her life-work crowned with success?
NEVER!
What can her motive be?

MONEY MONEY MONEY we actually hissed, then burst out laughing.

Scottie stood there with his index finger jammed onto the page like an unexploded shell.
 He will ruin us, Scottie. I must tell Mama. Wilfred is terrified of her.
 *He won't ruin us, Miss Maxwell. He hasnae got the slightest idea how the books work and is too drunk most of the time anyway, I am controlling the business as I've **always** done, just allowing him a little leeway.*
 My brother is a complete and utter idiot.
 Aye he is.
 I must tell Mama…

Of course, Maxwell's grand dame, The Mater, knew all about their doings. The whole of Weston-Super-Mare knew everything – though not always accurately, despite Scottie's best and most indiscreet gossip. I think that in her bleak way she had to approve of her son's involvement with this old 'gold-digger' as they saw 'Miss Morgan'. The whole of County as well as Town had always assumed her only son was a Nancy Boy. The powerful, irresistible tides of Town gossip whispered that her own husband, a former Admiral, had always been rather fond of having young matelots around and no doubt showing them how to tie knots and splice main-braces – whatever they might be.

I had never seen Maxwell Mater but rather imagined that she was impossibly old, veiled, haughty and devoid of any form of human, working-class understanding. Ethel told me that she lived her remaining life through her servants and saw things from on high, in the Upper Rooms of their extremely large house. With the use of powerful ex-Navy binoculars, she could easily see from the comfort of her armchair out toward Brean Down where strange things involving her strange son were obviously taking place.

 I meant to wave to her one day, when it was all done.
 In the meantime…

The day came when, as far as we could see, our rebuilding was complete – Moon Pyramids and all. They actually looked impressive, and certainly radiated their own electricities when the rising or setting sun proceeded down their little avenue either to or from the small Stonehengey portal the lads had thrown together. Viv – I had begrudgingly started calling her that by now – Viv said we would have a grand opening ceremony on a day that marked the 'Festival of Water' from the Old Country. From Atlantis, that is. Much of it would take place on the sea-shore. There would be music, dancing, singing and a general loosening of the spirits that she would orchestrate.

I still didn't pay much heed to all that Atlantean stuff she kept trying to hypnotise me about. It could have been on another planet as far as I cared. Any realm that was half-forgotten, lost, brimming with mad histories and filled with possible ancestors and monsters might as well be called 'Atlantean'. As I was never likely to learn the truth of my own biological origins (whether from darkest Cymru or greenest Somersetshire) Viv was welcome to think of us as 'Atlantean'. Anything was better than wearing the old school ties of Eton or Harrow.

Viv also added, quite waspishly:
And bring your little girlfriend to the Festival.
I assumed she meant Fleur. She read my mind.
***Ethel**, I mean.*
Can't I bring both? And shock the worthy folk of Weston?
If you must.
It's Fleur's birthday then.
***Is** it!? Hmmm... Yes. Yes do. Actually, it will be appropriate.*
She's never been to a party.
Then we must make it a day for everyone to remember, Our Divine Ancestor Khe-Ta will show especial interest.

I didn't care what tosh she was talking. She was probably on as many drugs as Maxwell himself by that time, but I liked the idea of giving Fleur a treat. Viv was flowing, though...
That Ethel woman...
Yes?
You're probably too besotted to notice, but she has a deformity of her spine.
Bitch, I thought.
You probably think me a bitch, but imagine the damage that does to her Visuddhi chakra, and thus to you.

*Ha! She tells me that **you've** got the thickest ankles she's ever seen. That you must have a problem with water retention that will soon cripple you. And that you have a constant smell of piss common to old ladies in nursing homes.*
Bastard.
We both are.

I never learned whose idea it was to send Fleur a birthday card. The little mite hadn't been well – her wheezing, coughing chest again – but the card was an actual tonic better than any of the Collis-Brown's Chlorodyne that we bought by the bottle-full over the counter at the local chemist.

That creature first known as 'Miss Morgan' did tell me some weeks ago that Maxwell was a truly talented artist but I had dismissed her comments. In fact, I never wanted to hear anything positive about him. I think this is what siblings do. Or perhaps, as the Priest of Moon whispered to me one night, I was simply jealous of him being Viv's lover. I banished that wretch instantly. To me, he/it, had no substance worth indulging on any level. Have you ever watched steam rising from a boiling kettle? He/it – the mighty Priest of the Moon - was no more than that, just a dampness on the brow if you let him/it near.

Yet… the card was beautiful. It showed a little girl in a walled garden, surrounded by sunflowers. The girl has long red hair like Fleur's, a flowery dress like the one Ethel bought her and bright red boots – just like hers. The letters, big and bold as anything from some Illuminated Gospel, wished her the happiest of happy birthdays and invited her to a party.

The card was, you will agree, wonderful, but I should have stopped Fleur from seeing it and quickly burned it then scattered the ashes far from our house. I can't help thinking it might have had some malign sorcery in the lines and colours that led to what followed…

Our work on the Fort was done and we had been paid extra and - I will admit – rather handsomely. Tom, Dick and Harry with their pockets full of cash and minds full of interesting memories and gossip would have disappeared into the shells of their quiet lives like the small hermit crabs that hide on the Weston and Brean sea-shore. Or they would have done if it hadn't been for that drug-dealer known as Beardmore.

I suppose that I should, as a law-abiding man serving King and Country, say something about that drug-dealer's death. I use the words 'say something about' carefully, and also the word 'death'. Others might say: 'confess to' and 'murder', but that is twisting reality. Beardmore's death was caused by the sudden impact of his body on the rocks below the cliffs. It was Earth that killed him, not us.

The lads had collected the remains of their working gear and were strolling back into town from the Fort. I was slightly behind them. It was a glorious day, and if the short-lived bluebells had withered the slopes were alive with White Rock Rose and Somerset Hair Grass, and enough daffodils for Penry to have soothed Penry's homesick soul. I suppose that Beardmore was making his way up to the Fort on his motorcycle to give Maxwell his next fix; I had heard gossip from Scottie that he had been banned from driving it. For whatever reason – and I never did ask the lads – he was having a go at them on what used to be the hair-pin bend that we had so carefully and laboriously straightened. Beardmore's insults were from the vicious realms of his imagined upper-classness: My lads were branded as scum, bastards, idiots, worthless human rubbish who had damaged his precious machine and - ye gods - they were going to suffer. Didn't they know WHO he was!

These lads had fought for their country. They had seen Hell. They had protected the likes of Beardmore (safe within his town house and country clubs and lodges) from demons beyond the sea. Even the officers in their Regiments would not have spoken to them like that.

I will never blame Tom for striking Beardmore with the heavy plumb rule he had used in our labours. It missed Beardmore's forehead but caused him a glancing blow to the right temple, and so he sank to his left knee. Almost at the same moment Dick used his builder's level to slash at him, causing Beardmore to sink onto his right knee. Perhaps they should have stopped then but Harry used his maul to strike a heavy blow to the forehead. Yet none of these three blows were done with any strength. They were more token assaults, knowing that the full powers of the Crown would always support *his* like against *their* like. By this time, I was level with them. Beardmore saw me through his blurred eyes and staggered upright. Perhaps he thought I was coming to the rescue and would give my toughs a 'sound thrashing', as his sort used to term it. But his legs were not steady and his balance had gone. I was standing at the very edge of the road. I could have steadied him as he staggered toward me uttering an obscene Word. I could have stopped him. Yet I stepped aside without touching him and he lurched forward and over the edge, falling silently onto the churning waves far below.

Oops, said Tom.

He deserved it, said Dick.

We stood there, the lads and I, peering at his body far below, already being washed and sloshed like a starfish by the powerful tide, and then sinking completely.

What now Sarge? asked Harry.

It was clear as day.

Now the bike, I said.

They understood.

I pushed that over. We watched it crash on top of where he had been with a mighty splash. It could have been one of the grey seals down there or a mermaid.

Then the silence, the breeze over the grasses, the pure and innocent sky.

Now we go home lads. We say nowt. He must have lost control of his bike. We didn't see him. Got it? We. Didn't. See. Him.

And so we went. [16]

---

[16] Steele seems to unwittingly describe the Masonic ritual 'murder' of Hiram Abiff.

The lads were cheery as anything at the knowledge their old Sarge had sorted out a small problem. They knew I would keep them safe. We marched in step and by the time we got to the bottom of the hill and went our own ways, they were singing 'Roll out the Barrell' and 'It's a Long Way to Tipperary'. It was just like the good-old bad-old Army days amid the trenches.

Did any of us feel guilty?

How could we have even a dew-drop of compassion or a whisper of guilt? During our years in the rhyne-like, flooded trenches of Flanders, after massive bombardments, we had each of us held in our disgusted, horrified hands the assorted body parts of our once-perfect pals. We had overseen the deaths of tens of thousands of good men and true at places like The Somme or Passchendaele. All because of our attempts to stem the relentless German tides and bring peace to our own land under our own King and Queen.

Feel guilty about Beardmore? No, never. He was a drug dealer. I could see no possible justification for his existence.

And so...

I should have trusted my feeling about that party. My feeling was that Maxwell's invite should be ignored. This was not guilt. I had done nothing wrong, or unjust. Besides, Maxwell was so doped-up he was unaware of his dealer's non-appearance, and the man's body was swept away and curled around by tides and finally found between the legs of the eight-legged lighthouse at Burnham, and it was another couple of days before he was identified.

I wanted nothing more to do with 'Miss Morgan' and her worshipping puppet, but I felt that I was in a kind of smog. It reminded me of the times during the War when I had used phosphorus shells to lay down a smoke screen for when our lads and the tanks attacked. Once, the wind had changed and the nasty, white, misty stuff flowed back onto us. Our troops advancing across No Mans' Land would have lost all sense of direction, so the colonel ordered us to put on our gas masks, abandon the attack, and remain in place while feeling disoriented.

I was disoriented then. I wanted to 'stand down' and stay put, but Fleur kept waving the birthday card like a flag. Could you have denied the little mite?

Had my sister, in her role as Maxwell's 'Sea Priestess', done something to create a mental fog? I called her a phoney to her face, but behind her back I would have to admit that she could do these things.

Could *I* have become my own Earth Priest and driven this miasma away? Yes, oh yes I could. But I was in the thrall of being a Dad. Fleur had removed my own powers by whispering 'Dad Dad Da**ddy**, Oh Dad Dad Da**ddy**...' as she hugged me and exploded her own white phosphorus of excitement all around me at the thought of the party. Being otherworldly, a changeling, she had never had human friends. No-one had ever invited her to a party before.

And so we went, Ethel driving us up there in her little motor with a very tiny rear seat. When we got there Fleur jumped out like a jack-in-the-box and ran to hug the man who had invited her, but coughing loudly because of her chestiness. He shrank back.

She's not infectious! snapped Ethel before I could.

Viv looked at us both, assessing our relationship. Her red lips curved upward into a taut bow. Was she jealous!? I hoped she was.

Ah so this is the little Mongol, was Vivien's comment.

Her name is Fleur, I snapped.

*Of **course** it is, your own Flower Lady. Actually, you should have called her Blodeuwedd.*

For a moment I was back in school with her and Carstairs was telling us about 'Blodeuwedd', the woman created by wizards out of nine flowers, though I can only remember three: oak, meadowsweet and broom. Viv could 'see' us back there, together, side by side, children ourselves. I know she was reading my thoughts.

I think that Ethel over-heard or inner-saw, if there's such a thing:

*I must tell you Miss Morgan, that you pronounced it the English way, as **blod wed**. Whereas - of course - it should have been more akin to **blod-ey-weth**.*

Should it reeeeeally, Miss Maxwell. Well, there you go! Live and learn.

My feelings for Ethel rose at that. The two women seemed to be doing the 'Like Poles Repel' thing, but I couldn't see anything 'Like' about them. I felt it might turn out to be a good morning after all. But as an old soldier I maintain a secret cave in my mind where I can lock away things from the likes of Viv – and myself. I didn't want her seeing what happened to Beardmore.

I was prepared to be totally, but silently hateful toward our hosts, so as not spoil the day for Fleur. It was as though I had a live shell stuck in the chamber that needed either firing or removing, but Maxwell's gracious gift to my daughter completely disarmed me. Beautifully wrapped, with a big red ribbon tied in a bow, he got onto his knees and handed her a heavy box. She danced, she chuckled, she shone.

Open it, said Maxwell, surprisingly gently, and at the sound of this I felt a bit of a shit for thinking him a complete shit.

It was full of sweets. I'd heard gossip that in the days before Miss Morgan he had nuisanced the young woman behind the counter of the Bon Bon Box. I say 'nuisanced' rather than wooed, because he was twice her age. Besides, she had already done the rounds with Tom and Harry and god knows who else. But, from whatever motive, she did him proud here. The box was full of aniseed Black Jacks, Chocolate Soldiers, Sherbet Fountains, pink and yellow Fruit Salads, gum drops, pear drops, gob-stoppers, peppermints and Liquorice Allsorts.

What do say, Fleur?

Thank you.

Having a sweet tooth, I snaffled three of the beady Allsorts when she wasn't looking. Now what do I say to this oddest couple of hosts?

Thank you, Mr. Maxwell. And Miss Morgan.

You're very welcome Mr. Steele. Now come indoors and join us for drinks and nibbles, eh? what?

That next half hour at the Fort is now little more than a blur. I suppose a 'blur' is what Beardmore saw in his four seconds of plummet: the flashing grey-black rocks of the cliffs; the black-blue of the roaring sea. Looking back, I wonder if The Vivien had wrapped me in one of her spells. I only have a sense of being in the room that had Maxwell's huge mural of dolphins and undines and sea-snakes and sunken galleons and galloping sea-horses and the rather sneering 'Priest of the Moon'. All those were drug inspired and so – in my mind – of no more value than the sugary sweets I was still sucking on.

Had *these* been drugged!? I certainly didn't feel 'right'. The ground beneath, normally so solid, seemed to be quivering. This area did – *very* occasionally – get slight earth tremors that did no more than rattle the windows and the crockery on the Welsh dresser. That was not what it felt like. Rather than credit Vivien with any real power, I'd rather blame it on drugs.

Wilfred and Ethel were arguing quietly but viciously. I remember her words to him: *Sly, nasty, lying* - among others. He raised his fist but realised that I was here, so slid it back into his pocket. I might have given him a warning now that I was no longer dependent on him for money, but then I heard – all three of us heard - a burst of Direct Voice from the spirit realm that exploded into the word **M'SIEUR!**

It was Astrid. She was always formal, as French people of her age often were. I was more often *M'sieur* than *Daniel*, and I often called her *Madame*. There was shyness in our use of names, for we were both oddities.

I turned toward the explosion of sound and saw through the big expanse of plate glass that ran down the side of the room…

Fleur.

Alongside Vivien.

Vivien was bent crone-like to walk hand in hand with my little girl, who was coughing. Then this sea-witch sister of mine stopped and stooped a little more. She whispered something in Fleur's ear. My daughter started to turn, perhaps to look for me. Her eyes were wide with fear. *Fleur!* – I started to shout, through the glass, when a huge grey wave folded over her like a blanket. As it withdrew, she was dragged on her bum over the greasy rocks and into the sea.

FLEUR! I roared and pushed Maxwell aside to dash outside. *NO NO NO NO NO!* when I saw her disappear below the waves.

Vivien half-turned when she saw me coming. I might be imagining the next but her eyes seemed to shine like cold lamps, each flash a different choice of a differing future that depended on what she did in the next second as I bore down on her. Then she waded straight into the waves, waist deep, was flung to one side by the strength of the tide but reached below the surface and pulled out what I thought was Fleur's bare leg, but was a stem of sea-fucus. I remember, as if in slow motion, slipping on the rocks and the rage I felt that my pure and solid Earth was compromised by the Slick and dirty Water of my sister. I was almost upon the spot, screaming when Vivien dipped below the surface again to pull my daughter out, whole and soaked, terrified and breathing heavily.

Here... she told me, cold as frozen water. Cold as though I had spoiled something.

Enough of this 'party', said Ethel, as warm to me as 'Miss Morgan' was cold. *Enough of this **nonsense!***

Vivien le Fay Morgan – or whatever it was she called herself – might have been a Sea Priestess from lost Atlantis but she stood no chance against a real human woman like Ethel.

Fleur was shaking, terrified. Perhaps in her endless churning seconds she had glimpsed monsters beneath the waves.

The hospital, Ethel. Now!

I sat holding Fleur as she shivered all the way down the hill, going into one of her torments. Wet as a seal. Short, rapid breaths, rapid pulse and evil cough. Saying she had pains in her side. I knew these symptoms only too well.

Ehtel drove us to Ashcombe House on the edge of Weston and she drove us *very* fast. At one point, after overtaking a horse and cart on a narrow road and coming out of a skid with calm skill, she gave me a Look. I knew that, in a differing way to my sister, she had also read my mind. She explained:

I drove ambulances in Flanders.

I didn't know that.

There's more to me than Friendly Girls.

My surprise was praise in itself.

Fleur, in my arms, wet and sea-stinky and slippery as a mermaid, looked dreadful. Yet I believe that the shock of the immersion – or attempted murder – simply brought to the boil what was already brewing.

I knew this hospital well. It was originally a small lunatic asylum, connected with Glenside in Bristol and had a small number of beds for those suffering from shell-shock. After the casualties of the Big Push now known as First Ypres, it was expanded into a specialist hospital treating the effects of mustard gas, as well as offering surgery for gunshot and shrapnel wounds. I had spent a month there myself for the latter, and the deep green peace of Somerset after the muddy hell of the trenches almost broke me.

The specialist was Doctor Rupert Malcolm, well-known for his aggressive manner to civvies, but kind enough toward me as he removed several vicious, crescent-shaped pieces of 'Stielhandgranate' from between my ribs. He had suggested, with heavy humour, that I could use my skills to fashion these into a necklace for my wife. Alas, Astrid died before I could make such a savage offering. I've still got the pieces.

I can talk calmly now, but that drive, following the shock of her near drowning, was a true dark morning of the soul.

Fleur was always prone to what they called 'Infections', that no-one really understands even now. Apparently, these were caused by bacteria in the nose or throat. Doctor Malcolm had gained some prestige and my eternal thanks by treating Fleur with some rich serum therapy that helped clear away her poisons and other things. Despite his reputation in the hospital he seemed to take to Fleur. His granite-hard, granite-grey face softened as he leaned over her cot bed the first time he saw her.

Hmmm...another ginger, like me. Do you want to be in my gang, little hunkypunk?

I've since learned that a lot of experiments were done on children like Fleur, on the assumption that they were less important beings and less fuss would be made if the experiments went wrong. In Fleur's case he mentioned that the serum he developed came from horses, but that was beyond my rank and need to understand. As long as it worked...

With all my head and heart, I willed Dr. Malcolm to **be there now!** and **on duty!** As Ethel drove, I held Fleur and sort of travelled along deep underground rivers that cut through the secret strata of Earth Time and pushed my mind into the best possible future. I created a picture of me and Fleur some months hence, playing in the sun, and remembering – making myself remember in the vision - how Malcolm had been, by pure chance, there and on duty, and how relieved we both were. That's not easy to explain. I've used it a few times, in extreme moments, and it got me through the War. But this was far more important.

Within ten minutes, no more, we pulled into the grounds of the hospital and the car skidded on the gravel forecourt. I was surprised to 'see' Sir Edern, son of Nudd, standing there quite cheerfully this time, dressed as though for a picnic, in the vibrant Earth colours of the coming months.

Summer is a-cumen in his manner seemed to say, and I knew that he was telling me something, that things were in place for us, and not to worry. But I also knew that beings like Sir Edern have forgotten the pains of earthly life or never known them.

Ridiculous, Sir Edern. You've never been a Dad.

Ethel almost ran into him because she didn't 'see' as I did. And then, stepping through the spirit as though Edern was a door, came Rupert Malcolm himself.

Oh! Hello! said the good doctor with surprise, almost getting into our car. *I thought you were my taxi.*

He told us later that he had been waiting for a cab to take him to a new post in a top London hospital. When he saw us, he dropped everything and gave Fleur (his former patient) his full attention.

Now that she was in good hands and I felt confident she would pull through, I made mental calculations as to how I would pay for the hospital stay, the cost of the serums and the doctor's own fees.

Yet...

Dr. Malcolm waived the latter. Fleur had been, after all, one of the first trialists of the system that made his name.

And Ethel insisted on paying for everything else.

We had an argument, based upon my 'manly' pride, but she stopped this with the sharp comment: *I've got **plenty** of money, Daniel. And besides, I **love** that little girl.*

I felt, but didn't 'see', Astrid beaming.

Dites merci, m'sieur, I heard her tell me, quite sternly.

Merci, Ethel.

She seemed touched by my manner.

De rien, mon ami...

I wonder if Sir Edern from the sacred hill of Brent Knoll had a part to play in all this. In fact, I wondered if Sir Edern, tired of all the gurglings from the Priest of the Moon, had decided to step in with his own version of *Actually...*

Three nights and three days... Dr. Malcolm put her in a private room and injected her at 8 hourly intervals with the special serum that won him futures at the London teaching hospital. If it did come from horses I prayed that it might also invoke one of the Horse-Goddesses that Carstairs told us about. I forget the name... Rhiannon? Didn't her name mean 'silver wheel' or something? I wasn't listening at the time, being too eager to get out onto the hill amid the Misty People and the knowing glowing spheres of earthlight and learn from Sir Edern about the powers within the Earth.

She was surrounded by huge oxygen cylinders that looked so uncannily like howitzer shells that I wondered if Powers were trying to sneer at me. I had allowed that drug-fiend Beardmore to plunge to his death because of his use of needles, yet the same tool was keeping Fleur alive.

Ethel refused to leave and so we worked shifts to sit over her, making sure that one of us held her hand at all times, and also that the machineries and their tubes and electrical batteries with wires did what they should.

Fleur was frail at best, but she looked worse now, like a thin flake of broken flint. We worked shifts, taking turns to crash out in a big winged armchair that Malcolm hefted into the corner of the room, along with some itchy, heavy hospital blankets.

There was a moment, when Ethel was asleep, that I entered into my own personal realm of Deep Earth and its dark options. I kept reliving

Vivien's face when I ran toward her, when she seemed to be considering a million 'What ifs'...

Perhaps Vivien, my twin, was sending me ideas by telepathy, or it might just have been my own guilt. Buried within my personal darkness I had a fierce to-and-fro that tore me apart. It went something like:

Dan, Danny, Daniel, what if Fleur had drowned?
I would be shredded. My life would be pointless.
So you wanted her to live for your sake, not hers.

I gasped. That was vicious shrapnel she had blasted into me. It was also true. Fleur could have been running in the Summerlands with her starry mother.

Dan Danny Daniel... what future will a Mongol have in this day and age? She's already rejected by the world. No friends, no school, no chance of meaningful work when she gets older except – at best - as a skivvie in some hateful House.

I felt a clutching at my heart, my breath came heavily. She – or me - spoke the truth. I should have let Vivien *fail* to save her in the present in order to save her from the future.

And you are old, dear brother mine. You are likely to die before her. What then? Who would care for an Idiot?

Then I heard Astrid's voice from the purity of stars sweeping aside the dirtyness of Vivien:

Peace... M'sieur, now is NOT the time for Fleur to join me.

I jumped because a cold hand touched my brow. It was Ethel, who seemed more concerned about me than Fleur, who was now sleeping deeply and peacefully for once. I had forgotten what she had said about the Powers of Touch, but I felt it now as things fell away.

Daniel, I have an idea. I, or perhaps we, will found a small school that will cater for children like Fleur. Children from ordinary families.

It seems that she had been looking through the firm's books and something perfect had come on the market, in Brent Knoll of all places.

Had she read my mind when her hand stroked my brow? That did not matter. She was using the future to heal my present.

M'sieur, said Astrid before she dissolved. *Dites oui!*

Oui, I said, shaking my head free of airbursting thoughts, *Oh very much oui! And merci! Merci!*

Though whether I was thanking Astrid for her work below the surface, or Ethel's efforts above the surface, or even the Arianrhod, the silver wheeling Goddess spinning from beyond the stars, I couldn't have said.

We took turns sitting by her bed, never leaving her alone. When it became clear that she would pull through, Ethel dashed home briefly and returned with Maxwell's 'Secret Journal' that we had read through in previous weeks with not-so-secret delight. She had book-marked some pages with strips of notepaper.

*Daniel, look at these, listen to his absolute cheek, his words about the 'exceptionally Itless breed of females around Weston', and how useless **I** am. But but **but** – listen to this next...'Every place that is intended for a sacred edifice, **always** demands a life in its building...' And then this: '...a temple **always** demands a life in its building'. And listen, oh **listen**... '.... the cold sea-cult of the primordial deeps required **living** sacrifices'!! Then even more comments about sacrifice, sacrifice and more bloody sacrifice – Pardon my language!*

I was not surprised.

Ethel, I've begun to think that they tried to sacrifice Fleur.

Didn't the Morgan woman save her though?

When I look back, I think she actually pushed her.

(Or caused a wave to knock her over?)

I wonder if she tried to drug me. It was only your argument with Wilfred that stopped me gorging on those Allsorts. Once they took effect she would have ensured that Fleur was properly drowned

Oh Daniel, surely not. You've been reading too much of that book on Psychology. What do they call it...Paranoia?

I haven't. And I'm not para-wotsit. You don't understand my sister. My twin. My other self.

*I don't believe she **is** your twin sister. I think everything she says or does is false. Didn't you tell me that your old teacher was a notorious joker?*

Fleur stirred. We sat on either side of her cot holding her hands. She smiled at us and then into the shadows.

Au 'voir I heard Astrid whisper, and knew the danger was over.

Just assuming you might be right, will they try to get her again?

No, Ethel, the danger is past.

I knew that, and I knew why. Though his body had not yet been found, I suppose the temple *did* get its sacrifice in the form of Beardmore. Once Maxwell and Vivien knew that, they would have no need of Fleur. Though they would still have to face *my* reckoning: those days of human or animal Sacrifice should be long gone.

***How** do you know?*
***I know**, Ethel...*

The day that Fleur was pronounced fit and well and discharged into our care **should** have been filled with airbursts of delight into the dimpsey Somerset sky. Yet it became a day more akin ro mustard gas and choking madness.

Ethel and Fleur and I stood outside the hospital holding hands, ready to leave once we'd said goodbye to Dr. Malcolm. For some reason I remember the sharp sounds of the gravel crunching under my boots and the feel of fragments wedging into the cleats. The Earth was trying to warn me but I didn't listen. Have you ever had the sort of day when you find yourself treading through a minefield? The sky could be pure, the fields green and rolling, the birds singing lustily and there's nothing to indicate that malign forces had been laying mines underfoot - laying them so skilfully that no-one could detect them until they explode and blow your world apart.

Dr. Malcolm himself came to wish us goodbye. If I'd had the nerve to adopt some of the customs of the French, I'd have hugged and kissed him and sang 'The Marseillaise' in gratitude. 'God Save the King' might have been more appropriate though still daft. 'God Save Rupert Malcolm' was what I *really* meant. Or even, 'The Doctor *is* God'. Those who have had a child saved will know that this is not absurd.

Instead I gave him the firmest and longest of handshakes and uttered the deepest of thanks: thanks that went down through the crust, the mantle, the outer and inner cores and all those other unknown and unseeable layers until they get to the burning iron-nickel Sun at the very centre of the world.

He looked into my eyes as I spoke. I think he saw into a small crack in my soul. In return I held his gaze, his grey-green eyes, the aureole of greying red hair like the Archangel Michael who was supposed to guard the church at the Knoll and I felt he was the saddest man I'd ever seen.

Slow, lizard blink from his hooded eyes, hiding pain.

Faster blinks from me, firing through his irises for information.

I'm going off to London now, Mr. Steele, to tell the big-wig surgeons there exactly where they're going wrong.

I nodded. The gravel was crunching madly under the soles of my boots. I failed to find the right words and nodded again. To me, he was up there with Field Marshall Sir Douglas Haig. As a mere sergeant, a non-com, I didn't know how to express myself 'upwards'.

He stooped to Fleur.

Goodbye little hunkypunk he said, as though he knew about her other side. He was bending over, his big hands on his knees, his body a question mark. *You have a star around you, but I think you know that.*

She nodded. She was shy. She was silent. So was Ethel, who was sometimes cowed by 'class' as Fleur was by 'normal' people.

And then to me:

If you're ever near Charing Cross Hospital then do pop in. I will always find time for gentry such as you.

He didn't mean it of course, but people in those days did the polite and made such noises. Then his chauffeur pulled into the grounds of the hospital at the wheel of rather a posh Wolsey Tourer befitting his status, although I personally thought he deserved a Rolls Royce at least. The driver gave three bursts of throat-rasping noise from the horn you could imagine being made by a pterodactyl. He also gave me a wave and a quick wink! With the chauffeur's uniform and peaked cap, I didn't recognise 'Tom' at first in his new job. He winked again then looked straight ahead, dutifully. Our secrets would always be buried.

I noticed in the back of the car a very frail, sad, grey-faced woman wrapped in heavy blankets. Her expression was sour, devoid of hope. I gave her a big smile, wanted to tell her that if anyone could cure her, Dr. Malcolm could – and would.

He saw my expression.

She's not a patient, that's my wife, I heard him say, though I'm not sure if he actually said it out loud or if I read his mind.

The Wolsey drove out through the gates and the very next second a large black vehicle came bursting in through them. For a moment I remembered something Astrid had told me about the 'Ankou' from her part of France: one of Death's henchmen who wanders the Earth in his large black coach collecting souls.

How daft, I thought, but pulled Ethel and Fleur out of its direct line just in case. It scrunched to a sudden halt on the cursed gravel with a sound like fingernails on a blackboard and I saw the sign above the number plate: 'SOMERSETSHIRE CONSTABULARY'. I realised with a cold clutching of my heart that this was actually a Black Maria, used to transport prisoners. And that the two policemen inside were looking directly at me.

Guilt guilt guilt. This had to do with Beardmore. Of course. Were the Theosophists right when they whittered on about 'karma'? Some of the nurses had been gossiping about the body that had washed up the previous day. The whole town knew who it was despite a face, they whispered, that was half-eaten by the conger. Apart from his drug-addled customers, the whole town despised him.

Perhaps this was entirely innocent. Had I broken any windows on my other jobs? Was it old Arthur Chichester complaining about his wall? Or something to do with Muckley the Butcher, with whom I had a slight falling out some weeks ago?

I never touched him. I. Never. Touched. Him. I had no Word to offer them about that.

But… could I betray the lads to protect my future with Ethel and Fleur?

The driver stayed behind the wheel and the sergeant got out. He looked at the little cap badge of the Royal Field Artillery that I wore over my heart as a kind of medal and decided I would be no problem. I looked at the three-bar chevron with small crown on his arm that showed his authority and knew I was in trouble.

He was a Special Constable. They appointed a lot of those in the War to safeguard water supplies from German infiltrators. Or that was the idea. That sounds unlikely now but it felt like a major threat in those days. Poison our water and the War would be lost on the Home Front. Since then these Special Constables had all sorts of other responsibilities, not least catching villains.

I had faced wave after wave of field-grey German 'landsers' and even their elite 'Sturmtruppen' infiltrating from behind our lines and known exactly what to do. This somewhat overweight, jowly, soft chap from the lush and quiet fields of Somerset had me paralysed.

It was Ethel who spoke. She had no idea of the terrors dancing across my brow.

Can we help you Sergeant?
I was glad she said 'we'.
Daniel Steele... the burly sergeant said.
He wasn't asking. What could I do but nod.
I'm here to take you in for questioning.
I didn't ask what for. Perhaps I should have done. Ethel did, and the Sergeants' answer confirmed my worst fears.
He's been accused of murdering the Right Honourable Percy Beardmore.
Ridiculous! By whom?
Er, actually, by your brother, ma'am.
Stuff and nonsense! My brother's an idiot.
I said nothing. Perhaps I should have done. Could my silence be construed as guilt?
 Ethel looked at me.
I looked at her.
On my life, Ethel, on Fleur's life, I never touched him.
That's enough for me, Daniel...

I felt that I had been ripped apart and my pieces scattered across the world. Even now I can't think of the following events in easy sequence but they went something like this: the Ankou-Sergeant and his Black Maria; the Jail; the clanging cell-door that sounded like one of my cannons; the Accusations; the Lawyer; the Scorn; the shame; the loss of Fleur – and Ethel! - and the thought of the Rope.

And weaving through all of these worlds I seemed to hear Viv whisper: *There is a door without a key*. Well, that meant nothing to me. Was she telepathing a message? Was it a gloat? Was it advice? I think I saw that phrase in Maxwell's Journal but could anything good come from their workings at Brean Down? And then – I can tell you now - and **then** the arrival of a Being so great that these storms were calmed as though someone had said 'Peace, be Still'.

After two days of murderous silence that door without a key to my cell was opened by a very large brass key that squealed in the lock like a slaughtered pig. I was escorted by the Special Constable (almost respectfully) to a large room overlooking the Grand Pier, with distant views of the Down. There was no sign of the miles of mud because the tide was high, up to the promenade. Small fishing boats bobbed in the bay attacked by a million cackling gulls that sounded like Lewis guns.[17]

In the room behind a long table was a Sergeant and a Chief Superintendent - or whatever was the equivalent of a General in the Police Service. Next to them were three civilians in formal suits and bow-ties with bowler hats on the table in front of them like the tumuli on the Knoll. I would have imagined they were part of the legal proceedings but they exuded a quite different air.

Then there was Maxwell and his solicitor hunched at the far end. I never did get the learn the solicitor's name. Both seemed to be drowning. I immediately thought of the film being shown in town that week about a vampire called Nosferatu. A young girl who worked in the office with Scottie played the piano accompaniment for this silent horror. She told us how the audiences were divided between quiet terror or chuckling scorn. Maxwell looked like that creature on the posters: sallow, shrunken, bent, and ill.

I immediately expected him to play the illness card and get sympathy for his asthma, though I knew that without Beardmore giving him what they called 'a fix', his body was reacting. I later learned that the term being used was 'cold turkey', but if you ask me he was more cold and gasping fish than any kind of fowl.

Help me, I thought, sending my message down through the floor, down through the foundations, into the very rocks below, piercing down toward the Core and the Innermost Sun. I'm not sure if the room then filled with a very thin sort of luminous mist, or if Light was indeed rising. Or if I was just being desperately and insanely hopeful.

Someone came into the room behind me. I was about to turn but:

*Eyes **front**, Mr. Steele!*

And I knew that one of the civvies behind the table was high ranking Army. Or even Navy. Or even new-fangled Air Force. Perhaps they were a sort of unholy trinity of the Armed Forces to which I had once belonged.

I felt the vibrations on the parquet floor, one heavier than the other. There was a faint scent of lavender from behind me, so one was a

---

[17] A First World War light machine-gun.

woman. I knew that it couldn't have been Vivien. She was bizarre in that she only ever liked the perfumes of camphor or iodoform. The man behind me exuded the familiar and distinctive smell of the expensive cigarettes known as 'Light Rays', that the officers in the trenches smoked in preference to the cheap Woodbines issued to the Tommies.

Eyes firmly front and at attention, I could see from the raised eyebrows of the men behind the long table that a Power had clearly entered the room.

Mr. Steele, this entire meeting is 'sub rosa'. Do you understand what that means?

I did. I knew *exactly* what it meant. Carstairs often used this.

No, sir I don't. Please explain.

It means 'under the rose'.

I looked up, feigning ignorance.

*It means that **everything** here will **NOT** be spoken about, or written about, or discussed with anyone. It will remain **secret**.*

The Power behind me then spoke in a resonant voice over my head to the assemblage at the table. Every vowel of every word projected Old Money and Old Schools and Stately Homes and the British Empire on which the sun never set.

How old are your grandmothers?

Came their dutiful answers, from the two uniforms in particular:

1222.
3169.
1222.
4093.
7160.

I am not a Freemason but I knew they were giving the numbers of their Lodges, of which there were many in Weston-super-Mare[18]. If Maxwell had slimeyed his way into Freemasonry then I was finished. After a long pause, during which all sorts of things seemed to float in the air and make it dimpsey, he then spoke to Maxwell's solicitor.

Have you at any time travelled to the East?

Another Masonic term. I was doomed.

Er, no. I went to Swindon last week. Why d'ye ask?

---
[18] Those Lodges still exist.

Is your client travelling to the East?
Not to my knowledge!
I felt a glimmering.

Then there was a brief exchange in which the solicitor tried to make sense of these highly unusual proceedings but he was shut down by those three men of higher class and greater authority than he would *ever* know. The two policemen were entirely quiet. I believe that the only way for policemen to 'get on' in the world is by becoming Masons. So the whole room was against me.

Then the Power spoke again:
Mr. Maxwell, what is your accusation?
'Nosferatu' clutched his stomach, seemingly impaled by agonies, terrified of the Powers functioning behind me.
I saw that man Daniel Steele throw my friend Beardmore over the cliff.
Liar, I thought.
Now Mr. Steele, what is your answer to his accusation?
I was able to reply with truth and vigour:
He's lying. I never touched Beardmore! I give my Word.

This was the Big Moment for the solicitor, no doubt pre-planned and rehearsed. He took a deep breath and delivered it.
*I only ask this 'court' to consider one thing. Who would you believe? The Honourable Wilfred Maxwell, a man of substance who is a valued member of the upper classes in our society? Or would you believe this wretch known '**Mr**. Steele', who is no more than a mere carpenter!*

To which I heard a roaring *woman's* voice from behind me explode:
'AND SO WAS OUR LORD!!'
The best silk in England would have been silenced by that blast. A two-penny-ha'penny dead-beat like him just shrivelled.

Then the mysterious woman added:
*On the day in question, with my late husband's Royal Naval binoculars, I saw that drunkard Beardmore drive his dirty motorcycle too fast to take the bend up toward the Fort. I saw him plummet to the rocks below. There was no sign – I repeat **NO** sign - of Mr. Steele or anyone else for that matter.*

Wilfred Maxwell really must have felt a stake splintering through his cankered heart. He sank his head to his chest and croaked:

Mother, oh mother…
And effectively, from that moment on, I was a free man.

I left the court buildings on Walliscote Road and stood alone at the edge of the Marine Lake that they were building. They had created a concrete barrage between Knightstone Island and Claremont Crescent. The architect in the local rag boasted that it would be an 'infinity lake', whatever that might be, the largest of its kind in the world. Once finsihed it would have a diving stage, rafts, rubber boats, water chutes, and children's paddle boats. There would be hundreds of bathing tents and dressing enclosures. That sounded like the sort of project the 'Sea Priestess' would have adored. I wondered if she had been vamping the designers as well as Wilfred.

I stood and took several deep breaths and thanked the Powers Beneath while looking over to the glistening prick of 'Bell Head' that had almost shafted me. Was Vivien still there, posing in the Frenulum?

Two sides of me glared across. One of them was me as the dark Destroyer of Worlds who had every skill needed to destroy that whole place. But, as I actually trembled at what I had almost lost, the other side of me needed to be one of the Shining Ones, a Goody Two Shoes for the rest of my reborn life.

I felt a shifting in the air, a breeze from the land to sea and the smell of 'Light Ray' tobacco. Came that potent tone from behind:

You can turn around now, Danny Boy.

I did. This was my saviour! I was ready to kiss his feet if necessary. The man's powerful voice in the court and 'under the rose' suggested a tall, intimidating Captain of the England Rugby Team sort. Yet beneath the black three-piece suit and double-breasted waistcoat, this fellow was rather weedy. Even so, although his bowler was tilted at a silly angle there was something about his manner, in his eyes, that would make you follow him over the top and into No Mans Land when the whistles blew.

I looked him up and I looked him down.

You don't remember me do you?

Should I, sir?

Drop the 'sir' bollocks. You only ever called me 'Hey you!' at school.

At school?

*The. School. Our school, **ac-tu-al-ly** as Carstairs would say. At the Abaris!*

I was one of the little shits in the lower classes under the Missus. I don't...sorry, really don't remember many of the others.

No, you spent most of your time playing hooky out on the hill. You fancied yourself as one of King Arthur's knights. Or else you were closeted with that mad sister of yours and never let anyone near. You used to call me 'Sticky'.

I remembered the Cave Under the Hill, the arrival of the Sea Priestess, the minions around us all, the strangeness and the fires and the lostness of that realm and its aeons. I had a vision of the whole event that was both instant and endless and felt that this man had been part of it. I felt energies from Atlantis sweeping across the waves that were only from the Bristol Channel. I felt ten thousand years compressed into a single second.

I remember nothing, sir. Can I have a fag?

He smiled and offered me one from the silver case. As he struck a match I had another dual-life moment, remembering from the battlefields of Flanders that the first light from a friend's cigarette would draw attention, the second light provide an aiming point and the third light result in having a German bullet in your face.

We puffed away in silence. I think it was companionable. And then, as he pushed forward with his words cutting through like a driven plough. He offered:

Know! Will! Dare! - and above all Be Silent, 'Danny Boy', or the wrong sort of pipes will be a-calling you.

Did he mean be 'silent' about the very welcome travesty of justice that I had just benefited from? Or 'silent' about the whole 'Atlantean' Mysteries that had obsessed my sister and all those she enchanted? I think he had had the same burst of vision that Maxwell had evoked in the Secret Journal that everyone in town knew about. He wiped his brow with a silk handkerchief from his breast pocket and straightened his bowler. Then he came very close and gave me, a non-Mason, a strange handshake with a very sticky grip.

Go home, Danny. Enjoy your remaining years.

He turned a corner of the building and disappeared from my life.

I did soon learn his real name but won't tell you.

Well, there was more, but not much more. I had Ethel to thank for saving me. She had taken Fleur home and contacted The Mother and told her all.

In fact, Lady Maxwell knew more than most, thanks to the servants and the electric gossip of the Town gentry. She was glad to know that her son's drug dealer was no more, her only comment being:

Perhaps poor Wilfy might now have a chance in life.

Ethel was amused to tell me that the full title of the man with her was: 'The Most Worshipful the Grand Master of the Most Ancient and Honourable Fraternity of Free and Accepted Masons of England'. He was also the grand panjandrum of the – seemingly esteemed - Lodge of Agriculture from which the other Lodges in Weston were descended.

I didn't tell her that I had probably bullied him at school and called him Sticky. Or was it Stinky? I really didn't remember him. Perhaps he was no more than a seedling yet to sprout.

That was when I was invited to join 'Lady Maxwell' in her upper rooms. Note, I use the word 'invited' and not 'summoned' as would have been the case in earlier days. Ethel and Fleur were both there, playing dominoes in the corner of the large room with vast windows that looked toward the West. The sharp tapping of the pieces on the glass table were like the cracking of Lee-Enfields.[19]

And I realised then that the Power I had sensed entering the court room was not the Worshipful Master, but Ethel's tiny mother, who had her own agenda in coming to my aid and lying like a trooper. I had heard that she was a 'Dowager Duchess' whatever that might be. She was short and very slim, dressed from neck to ankle in dark blue silk. The irises of her eyes were coal-black, which contrasted oddly with the aureole of white, curly hair that seemed like a descending cloud on some mountain top. She radiated a sort of restless intelligence and I soon learned that she had a mind like a stiletto.

I think she liked me.

Then later, when Fleur was napping...

Mama, do you have sympathy for the Freemasons or believe in their creed?

No, Ethel dear, but I believe in blackmail.

What!?

---

[19] The Lee-Enfield.303 rifle was the standard weapon of the British Army.

*I own the deeds of the buildings they use on Tivoli Lane and other places. They owe a lot to your father and **his** pursuits.*
Papa was a Mason!?
She shrugged.
He was a lot of things. No-one ever knew exactly what he did within the Admiralty. Besides I was once – how shall I say it - very good friends with a certain Benny Cox. He used to come around when papa was away. Remember him Ethel? Benny?
Did he do card tricks? And prestidigitation?
That's the one! Magic hands, couldn't trust him. Sweaty, but clever. It all started with him, I suppose, when I suggested he used that octagonal room in the Duke of Oxford pub we owned. He founded the first lodge there, though he sometimes used the Three Queens Hotel when it got too crowded. Every Tom, Dick and Harry wanted to be a Mason in those days.

I could tell she was enjoying this. Doing a kind of Dance of the Seven Veils, revealing parts of herself never seen by her daughter - or anyone else - and being slightly shocking.

Strange name it had. 'Osiris'. Strange atmosphere in that octagonal room too. Yes, the Osiris Lodge. Mean anything to you, Steele?

I shook my head, but smiled. This was all a golden dawn for me after quitting the blackest of nights. After having had my life torn apart it had somehow been rebuilt and renewed because of things done in the past by men with aprons in that silly Osiris Temple.[20]

Fleur woke up, grizzling. Lady Maxwell pulled a face and Ethel decided she would take her to do some painting downstairs and annoy Scottie, who would be desperate for news. It was clear that Lady M wanted to talk about deep and troubling things.

Can unspoken thoughts form a cloud before the brow? Lady M had lied outrageously to save my life. She knew it, I knew it. The cloud – a glistening one – floated between us like one of the smoke screens that I would lay down across No Man's Land before our lads attacked and the tanks were unleashed. (Tanks that, because of the dangling six-pounder guns, all the lads called 'Big Willies'!)

---

[20] Benjamin Cox was a member of the Inner Order of the Golden Dawn, his 'Motto' being *Crux Dat Salutem*.

Let us adjourn to the upper rooms, Steele.

She led me up a flight of stairs to the very topmost room with spectacular views across to the Down. It was clear that with a good pair of binoculars, even just with good eyesight, she could have seen what really happened that day.

A servant wheeled in a trolley filled with neat triangular sandwiches and various cakes. I was starving after the lack of food at the jail. *Eat* was all that Lady M said, giving a slight gesture with her hand. So I stood and gorged on the triangles and didn't care what they contained.

She sat herself next to the window on a throne-like, winged chair, and pulled a large open book onto her lap. I've no idea what the book was. A Bible? Debrett's 'Peerage' - that most of her class ranked equal to the former? Or a list of all the properties she owned?

I was never in awe of the so-called Upper Classes, though unlike increasing numbers of my lads in the Regiment I didn't resent them. There is that part of me that was once a High King at Brent Knoll and that rather trumps a mere 'Lady', no matter how wealthy. Besides, years before I had been eye-to-eye with the Queen herself, though this one came from Denmark and not Atlantis.

As a young soldier my battalion had been paraded before Queen Alexandra, wife of Edward VII, who took a dutiful interest in our regiment. I was intrigued to see that, being deaf since her teens, she always used fingerspelling to communicate. I never learned it myself.

I think she was more than merely human. Perhaps they sensed her true origins among the stars. Or maybe she picked up energies from me! Parts of the country made a quite a cult of her.[21]

Our colonel was obviously smitten by her and had prepared a feast in the Officers Mess for the big-wigs

---

[21] The coal-mining town of Ashington named Alexandra Road in her honour for reasons no-one now knows. (The present publisher was born there and later moved to the adjoining Ariel Street, named after a faery – the street I mean, not me. Just sayin'.)

after the parade. He tried to hurry her along the lines of us mere squaddies but she took her time with us. She was a very attractive woman, with a marked and oddly fey presence that had nothing to do with this recently renamed 'House of Windsor'. She asked odd questions along the line and you could feel each lad glow. It amused us rankers to watch the Colonel with his clumsy sausage-fingers spelling out their answers and voicing them.

She came to me. Our eyes met. She frowned. A cold grey wind swept around us like a shroud. She smiled, leaned toward me and whispered:

I come from behind the North Wind.

I nodded. I knew **Who** she was. Did she know **What** I was?

I think she saw.

One day, corporal, a Great War will come.

Yes Ma'am.

Will you be ready?

I am now, Ma'am.

I learned later that because of Prussian conquest of Danish lands, she **loathed** the Germans. She may have been Deaf but she certainly wasn't Dumb. With a wicked smile she said in the ringing tones that Royalty affect:

*Jah! At ease then boys! Your Colonel has provided a feast in the Officers Mess for privates and N.C.O.s **only**. Isn't that right dear Colonel? Privates and N.C.O.s **only**. Do we have your word, sir?*

She used the Royal 'We'! and we loved her for it. The Colonel's face exploded with red. Deep breaths. Suppressing scowls. Then his fingers spelled, bitterly and slowly:

Y. E. S.

And the Queen winked at me. [22]

At. Me. Perhaps it was her influence behind the scenes that saw me made a sergeant the following week.

I thought of that moment on the bleak Salisbury Plain that was happening simultaneously with this one in Weston twenty years later but also Now. Looking at Lady Maxwell and trying not to stare or go 'absent', I could see her own grey-haired Power that had nothing to do with wealth. She was indeed as queenly as Alexandra. Perhaps she had also been present at 'Bell Knowle' when my sister had arrived from

---

[22] See the British Sign Language 'Finger-spelling Alphabet' in the Appendix.

'Atlantis'. I suppose even a High King then had to have a Mother somewhere.

I stopped eating and wiped my mouth with a napkin.

Sit down.

I sat down before her. I noticed the heavy chair was angled so that the road to the Fort was in full view.

You owe me, Steele.

I nodded.

And so, to business...

I raised my eyebrows.

My useless son is convinced that the Morgan woman has sealed herself into a cave within the Down.

That made a nice picture in my head but I gave her an instant response.

Impossible ma'am.

She could see from my face and tone that I knew every part of that Down and its Fort – above, within, below; past, present and future.

Dammit. I rather hoped...

I raised a single eyebrow.

She led him along.

I nodded.

I like your brevity Steele.

Ma'am.

You may not know it but the Morgan woman has disappeared.

I shrugged. Vivien did that sort of thing.

She stole a lot of money, not just from us but many tradespeople.

I gave her a look that said, without words, 'Not surprised'.

She stole furs and also my necklace of star sapphires.

Poor sapphires.

No need to jest Steele.

No ma'am.

I like sapphires. They are royalty. They come from the deepest layers in the oldest lands, far away from the thin, sticky mud of Weston. People think they are just blue, but they can come in every colour of the rainbow. The more intense and uniform the colour is, the more valuable the stone. I know these things. I'm sure they were traded when I was that King of the Hill. I've no doubt that my now-seen-as-wicked Sister must have felt they were hers by right and rite. I probably would have taken them myself given the chance.

I've been led to believe by Headley, our solicitor, that she plans to sell these in Hatton Garden in London. To pay for this 'glandular treatment' that's all the rage.

Glandular Treatment?

My first thought was of Rupert Malcolm.

My second thought was to Be Silent.

I am going to fund you, Steele.

Fund me, ma'am?

With cash. Adequate cash.

And then?

I want you to find this woman.

And **then**?

Get my star sapphires back. And the other bits of silver she took.

I looked out toward the glistening prick of Brean Down. It was very dimpsey and calm out there but thunderclouds were gathering across the Channel. They seemed to form into dark horses whose riders had wild flying robes and winged helmets ready to snatch up lost souls. I knew that gang only too well. I had faced them often enough.

Steele?

I came back to the Now. She was looking at me intently. Did she see where I go? Did she understand certain things?

After which, ma'am?

Kill her.

I enjoyed my train journey to London. Although I was more than adequately funded I was quite happy in Second Class, besides which Third Class was full, standing room only. In fact, I have always enjoyed being a passenger on trains, even when they packed us soldiers in like cattle on the way to the Front while the officers rode First Class and had tiffin brought to them on trays by their batmen. It was a feeling of being neither here nor there, neither coming nor going. I would almost go into a trance: aware of my surroundings but not quite present anywhere. There's probably a term for it in the book about the new-fangled 'Psychology' that Ethel kept dipping into.

I didn't tell her the full extent of my mission; didn't want her to think she was involved with a potential murderer. But then again, I had already killed tens of thousands merely by pulling a lanyard and shouting **Fire!** Yet could I – would I – kill my twin sister?

Vivien 'Le Fay' Morgan tried to drown my daughter as part of her mad, idiotic, ignorant brain-dead, drugged Atlantean magic.

So yes.

I could.

I had a lot to muse about on the train journey, not least the whole 'Atlantean' thing that seemed to obsess Maxwell. My sister was plainly hypnotising him.

Or...

Actually...

And that 'Or' and 'Actually' were bothering me. They were like shells stuck in the breech of the cannon, making it unable to fire; the exotic metals daring me to make a decision that might be fatal.

The light was behind us as we headed eastward, through the golden stones of Bath, once home of Abaris after whom my school was named – though he probably never existed. Then Chippenham, that once hosted the Kings of Wessex before 'England' existed. Then slowing into the monstrous Railway City known as Swindon, where it took on water and more coal, hissing like a beast in the process. I could almost feel the sentience in the steel and iron of its body, while the rhythmic chugging of the train and the clickety clack of the wheels on the tracks had its own sort of intelligence.

With the beginning of dusk, I saw myself reflected, silvery-grey and blurry, like an astral projection, in the windows at both sides of the carriage. And beyond me, through me, I glimpsed the flashing lights of stars moving in the indigo deeps of the Wiltshire countryside.

Were these more than reflections: perhaps aspects of myself in some parallel world?

Hello, I said to all of my reflections. I can't imagine they heard.

There was that logical side of me that knew Maxwell's adored 'Sea Priestess' did not come from the City of Golden Gates on the Isle of Ruta in lost Atlantis, but ***actually,*** as I keep saying, from somewhere in the countryside beyond Barry Island, in South Wales.

Then again, I looked at my parallel reflection in the window at the other side of the carriage and wondered whether Maxwell's use of the place-names Bell Head, Bell Knowle, Starber and Dickmouth had their own reality. And if so, perhaps their parallel realm *did* contain a Sea Priestess demanding sacrifice who really *did* come from lost Atlantis? I remembered Carstairs words: 'Everything that *can* happen, *does* happen.'

I must have dropped off to sleep. Or else had one of those waking dreams that are more than dreams. I certainly do not do the trance-work that all the back-street mediums seem to go in for when they're able to raise their astral heads above the legal parapets. At any rate I became aware of Sir Edern ap Nudd in the compartment with me. He seemed to have descended into the body of the chap sleeping opposite, unaware of being possessed, his head nodding with the rhythm of the train.

Daniel Daniel Danieeeel...

I heard it in my mind. The other travellers were getting their last few moments of doze before the terminus at Paddington.

*What great wisdoms have you got now, **Sir**?*

I didn't speak out loud – or don't think I did. And at that moment I wasn't sure if my use of the term 'Sir' was a reference to his knightly status or getting him confused with classroom memories of Carstairs. I suppose I was confused. The tension of the last few days had been immense and prospects for my future uncertain.

*Whether she is a real Sea Priestess from Atlantis or a modern actress playing roles is **not** what you need to worry about.*

What is?

That which you have buried within the deepest Fires of the Innermost Core of the Oldest Earth.

That annoyed me. Speak clearly, speak Human!

What!?

That you are, always have been and will be, in love with Vivien.

I burst out laughing. Forget all the Latin or the Greek 'Words of Power' that some bang on about in their Grimoires. Nothing will banish spirits better than laughter. That made him disappear like a popped balloon.

It also woke the others in the compartment. They looked annoyed. Fearful. One of them made a screwing gesture on his off-side temple to the man opposite, who raised his eyebrows and shook his head slightly.

The chap whom Edern had briefly possessed looked confused and shook his head and shoulders rapidly.

Where was I going – really *going* – with all this? Was it just repayment of a debt? I felt the little cap-badge I wore on my old great-coat and took comfort from the motto of the Royal Field Artillery: one of the few places where I felt that I belonged despite the butcher's bill. *Ubique* it said, meaning 'Everywhere'. But it also added: *Et Gloria Ducunt* that means 'Where Right and Glory Leads'. (Or so we were told. You can imagine the smutty fun the lads had with that very last syllable in our motto.)

Was I heading to Right and Glory here in this train to London? Perhaps personal feelings don't count in this sort of thing. Scanning through Maxwell's 'Secret Journal', that's exactly what 'Miss Morgan' told him, justifying her use and mis-use of him in terms of Magic rather than Morality.

Or maybe Ethel and I just read that piece wrong.

It is hard work always trying to be logical, and 'make sense' of the incredible. Sometimes you have to load and fire and load and fire, and trust that your aim is good even though you might never see the result.

But this Atlantis thing… It bothered me as much as it inspired that useless Wilfred Maxwell. It seemed that everyone and their maiden-aunt took Atlantis as Gospel. Or maybe it was just the upper-class circles in which I orbited when doing my earthly odd-job things, without which some of them could barely function.

They all seemed to have read that book by the American senator about Atlantis being an 'antediluvian' world. Well, that word 'antediluvian' – pre-Flood and all its wateriness - would have spoken to Vivien. But when I think of all those maiden aunt-type sex-deprived Theosophists who were never quite rich enough to be seen as Quality, or posh enough for 'Debrett's Peerage', then they were always going to see themselves as an alternative sort of royalty: Atlanteans reborn – and with a mission.

Many of them added stuff about Root Races. Certainly, 'Father Carstairs' spoke about these and often read out extracts in hushed tones As I recall, the Lemurians were the 3rd Root Race, and they evolved into the 4th Root Race of the Atlanteans, and then we appeared as the 5th Root race. By 'we' I mean thee and me: the ordinary folk. However, the Theosophists who were churning out all this stuff saw themselves as members of the emerging and highly evolved 6th Root Race that was emerging from California in particular, and the posher parts of London, around Harrods in particular.

Well, maybe it's all true - who am I to say they're wrong. But the '6th Root Race' examples I've seen at the local Theosophical meetings were a pretty duff lot, gaunt vegetarians prone to wearing sandals and open-necked shirts. I think that sort of thing about Root Races will cause trouble in the future, though I can't say or 'see' exactly how.

Young Vivien seemed gripped by this in class and totally absorbed. She always did like drama. My mind was too absorbed in daydreams about deeper things, within and below the Earth, and the 'giants' in the Knoll existing in the vast underground caverns found in deepest strata of Deep Time who had no interest in us mortals on the surface.

After my first encounter with these, and somewhat betwaddled, as they say, I heard the school bell ring from the slopes below, announcing the evening meal. I have always liked the sound of bells, even those from the dismal churches of dead religions. I especially liked to hear, from the Bristol Channel on foggy nights, the two tones of the warning bells on the Burnham lightship that cut across the treacherous waters and even into our rooms at the Abaris. The tones were known locally as the Cow and the Calf, and they kept mariners safe in their ships and us landlubbers dreaming in our beds[23]. It is the metal – usually bronze – that vibrates and agitates the air, pinning the listener to the moment and the place, making his world stop. Well, *my* world certainly did, I don't know about 'normal' people. The Abaris school bell was a great hand-held living creature that apparently came from a ship. It could easily smash your knee on the down-swing if you weren't careful. Carstairs, of course, confided to me that the vessel in question was the Flying Dutchman and that he had been its captain years before. I'd never heard of that ship and its story and had no reason not to believe him. It was some time before Vivien put me wise. I had to smile.

But, as I went inside the gates of the school it was Carstairs, 'The Father', who saw my shiny eyes and took me aside and asked me *exactly* what I had seen. So I said, *exactly*:

Giants...

His eyebrows rose. His brow furrowed. Behind the wrinkles were lines of thought.

---

[23] Steele is mistaken. They were not bells but two different-toned foghorns

They are Titans, Daniel. Titans.
What did I know? I buried the word under the rubble of my recent encounters and went in to supper.

And I was also getting inner 'nudgings' that seemed to come from Sir Edern ap Nudd when I was out on the crest of the hill itself who always had his own agenda. I didn't commune with him much during the War but I think he was never 'far' away. I believe he protected me in strange and subtle ways. I suppose his sort always have their own plans when they commune with us. I sometimes think they regard us as servants, and expect us to become costumed fools waving arms and weaving light to offer bring them spiritual tiffin.

The train steamed along: *iron an' steel, iron an' steel, iron an' steel…* it said to me. It became dark, with miles yet to go. Time for a fag and yet another lightning half-doze: an art I perfected in the Army – every soldier does. I don't often float off to sleep on trains, though many might think it relaxing. I like to sense the Earth and its pulses beneath – an infinitely slower rhythm than this clickety-clacking, fire-eating, steam-breathing and hissing monster of the Great Western Railway. – or 'God's Wonderful Railway' as the wags called it.

Thinking it through on the brink of a doze, I suppose that Carstairs might have suggested that 'Bell Knowle' is an otherworldly, perhaps etheric location that overlays Brent Knoll. And that Maxwell's vision, might have its own kind of truth. And so, in that realm, dear Vivien really *was* what he envisioned – a Sea Priestess who might make a man of him in his mother's eyes at least - and not just a confidence trickster who robbed him blind and helped him become an addict.

Does that make sense?
It does if you go down a rabbit hole.
It won't stop me killing her that I find when I do find her.

When we reached the terminus at Paddington Station, in the westernmost part of London, I spent a little time on the platform getting my bearings. For me, it was not just the points of the compass, but those points above and below and within. It was something I always felt, even as a young lad in the Army with the heaviest of boots: an energy, a 'nudging' that would creep up through the soles, up my legs and arse and spine, into the bottom of my brain. When I hear the

Theosophists banging on about this 'Om' thing, I can only compare it to the Deepest Earth sending me a pulse that said 'Hello'.

That must sound crass, but I'm not an intellectual - as Carstairs kept reminding me, to Vivien's endless delight.

Actually no, it's not crass. I just remembered Fleur's kaleidoscope! I got it for her last birthday, It's a brightly coloured tin tube with a series of mirrors and loose pieces of coloured glass inside. She aims it at the light, looks through the eyehole, turns the end, and the world becomes an endless series of patterns. I found it hypnotic. She had to wrestle it from me. The world and its souls transformed into endless, twisting, turnings of fragmented light glimpsed through random shapes and histories.

I suppose *that's* what it's like. I suppose that's what *I'm* like!

There. That's *definitely* the best I can explain. He who has eyes to see… If you're still not happy then I can only dismiss you with the immortal words 'Sand Fairy Anne'…

Yet even before that first moment of Earth-greeting, I would get ripples of the past. I felt it on my very first trip to London when I went to the recruiting office hoping to get accepted into the Coldstream Guards. As it was, they didn't think I quite had the 'you know what' for that august regiment. When they saw my background, they let me sign on but sent me straight to the garrison on Brean Down just five miles away from the Knoll! Well, some flow of Earth Consciousness clearly had plans for me even then. It was years before I understood what they meant by 'you know what', but by then I'd outgrown those bastards.

On that very first trip to London I had a sense of ancient fires and waves of death that quite shook me. Yet as I stood still (so still the Recruiting Officer behind the desk thought I was in a trance) I got a sense that these were ancient shock waves from Boadicea's pillage and destruction of the Romans who had raped her daughters. Now *that* was a Cause and a Woman – a **Great** Queen – I'd have happily fought for! Even now, I haven't quite forgiven the recently-formed nation of 'Italy' for the Roman slaughter.

It was not like that now, in my pursuit of the Sea Priestess: no fires, no terror and not even a hint of severed Roman heads. But despite the post-War weariness the slumbering power of the City was undeniable.

So how was I to find Vivien? Hire a Private Detective? Ask the Masons for help? Put adverts in the papers asking 'Have You Seen This

Woman - Reward'? Use a dowsing pendulum? That last might seem daft but I'd seen Maxwell and Vivien with a crystal one, and don't doubt that it can work. Although in her case I think she used the swinging cord to hypnotise him.

The answer to all of them is No.

Like a retreating tide, her life left patterns in the sand that offered clues. And one of them struck me forcibly that very last moment I came near Dr. Malcolm outside the hospital at Weston. With the subsequent immediate arrest by the constables, I had to push it aside until I was set free by the Powers of the Lodge and the Dame. Then it became obvious. The Good Doctor had on his person, suffused in his clothes, the smell of camphor. He would not have been using it on patients to relieve pain or itching; I knew at once that Vivien had been doing her vampire thing on him to relieve pain and itching of a different kind. That's why she disappeared from Brean Down, leaving the witless Maxwell to fancy she had become a timeless goddess within her cave, somewhere underfoot.

I was certain that if I found Rupert Malcolm I would find Vivien.

Maybe I could save him too.

To be honest, despite the crowds of Paddington Station, it felt like that moment of the 11th Hour of the 11th day of the 11th month in 1918 when the guns stopped and the world stood still and the silence was almost painful. Overlying that, *actually*, I allowed myself to realise that I was enjoying the world!

I had:

Avoided a Death Sentence.

Silver money was clinking in my pocket and large banknotes rustling in my wallet.

Knowledge that Fleur would be having the best time of her life in the good motherly hands of Ethel.

And I was in London and not Weston-super-Mud, determined to be a simple tourist for a little while!

Killing a Sea Priestess would be the least of my concerns.

London… I can never quite escape its gravity. I don't think anyone can. If you visit once, you have to go back, it's like doing a physical double-take. Carstairs told us that the name came from 'Llan Dian', or Temple of Diana which once stood where St. Paul's Cathedral is now. But he was always plucking things out of the air like that.

I remember a school trip to the long crescent beach at Brean Sands.

He kept picking up unusual stones, or shells, and telling stories about each one. He picked up a tiny shell that had an even tinier hermit crab inside, and gave us a yarn about what the crab told him. Something about pirates and Saint Patrick (or it might have been the Magdalen visiting her mother-in-law in Anglesey?) all told him by the minute creature he held to his right ear.

Vivien was having none of it.

You made that up!

Does it matter?

I was on his side in this.

He put the shell down on a rock. I saw Vivien go back later and throw it into the rising tide.

I spent that first night in The Smoke, as Londoners call it, in one of the 'Dis and Dem' lodging houses - for 'Discharged and Demobilized Sailors and Soldiers'. There were a lot of them around, and those men needed a lot of help. I felt a bit of a fraud staying there, being neither disabled nor in need of charity, but I needed a quick fix until I could get sorted.

Saying that, I probably sound like Wilfred Maxwell, who was always needing quick fixes of a different kind.

After checking in, I made my way across London to the British Museum. As I strolled along Great Russell Street toward the magnificent front with its soaring columns, it seemed to me more like a

Temple than any Temple I had yet seen. The whole place – in fact the whole area - was shaped from Portland Stone that had been layered on the Isle of Purbeck 150 million years ago, before even Lemuria and Atlantis were dreamed into existence and the most ancient beings lived on the planet Maldek[24] anyway - before it exploded. (That's another thing that Carstairs yarned about. Maybe a hermit crab had told him that too.)

As I approached the Museum I had flashbacks of Carstairs in our school, showing us a wide, black and white poster of its frontage and asking:

What is a pediment, Daniel?
I don't know sir.

I remember the hiss as Vivien's hand shot up like an Amatol shell from a Stokes Mortar.

A pediment is the triangular upper part of the Museum's front!

Well done Vivien! Though it can also be a sloping expanse of rock debris at the foot of a mountain.

He got to the point eventually, after several yarns about his cycling adventures, then showed us detailed drawings of the carvings:

The left side of the pediment of the British Museum shows primitive man emerging with difficulty from a cleft rock. There is an angel kneeling in front of him, holding a lamp and encouraging him.

As the London buses of 1922 scraped past me into the thickening fog I remembered Vivien's deep whisper from strata 30 years below:

That's me and you, Danny.
You're no angel.
You're definitely a primitive.

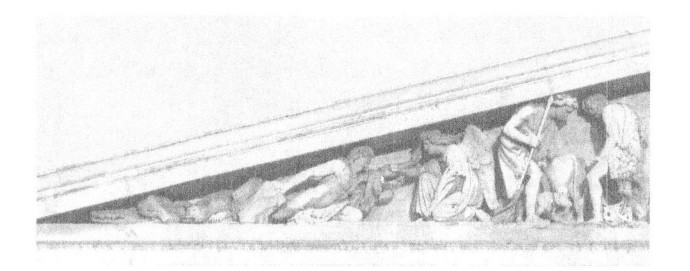

---

[24] Supposedly between Mars and Jupiter. It became the asteroid belt when it exploded.

Even now, it was the living qualities of the stonework that interested me. You wouldn't get anything like this from any watery, airy world created by any kind of Sea Priestess. I should have been a sculptor. I would have been a **great** sculptor, knowing how to listen to and shape the stone and make it even more alive.

Perhaps it was the Portland Stone flowing into me as I walked, but another memory from my Abaris school-days flared into my thoughts. It was a strange encounter with Mrs. Carstairs, my Foster Mother, who sat on the edge of my bed and gave me a photo. She whispered:

This is called The Veiled Virgin.

From her manner I thought it might have been a dirty postcard, a few of which Vivien had bought in Weston. I saw that this was just a life-size marble carving of a woman's head that someone had then covered with a thin veil.

No, Daniel, this was carved 200 years ago by Giovanni Strazza - from a single block of white marble.

Even then, it didn't hit me until she repeated the words:

Single. Block. White. Carved Marble...

I could not believe it. Then I **did** believe it.

I felt as shaky as if it really had been pornography. The actual subject meant nothing to me: I had no clear idea of what a 'Virgin' was. What I could not begin to understand were the human skills that could create such a thing from a **Single. Block. of Marble**. As a soldier I would spend a life blowing the world into fragments; but what wouldn't I have sacrificed to have this man Strazza's skill! Given the tools available even now, 200 years later, how was it even possible!?

This, to me, was a creation of pure magic.

This, to me, was Holy.

Thank you, I told her very softly, though I don't know why we were whispering.

People at the time said that Alchemy and Cagliostro were involved.

Actually, I did not doubt it. I could not and still cannot understand how any mortal could have shaped stone like this, to give it visible depths and seem covered by veils.

Keep this, Daniel. I have others, even one called the Veiled Christ - but don't tell your Father.

I never did.

I had read that later examples of 'Veiled Marble' were going to be on display at the Museum, hence my visit now. As I walked along the many-hued stones of London, I was Time Travelling with my 'Mother' and musing on the other veils that might cover us – mine in particular.

The Museum was still open for another couple of hours. There was electric lighting in the Front Hall, the Reading Room and in the Forecourt, but the heavy fog from a million coal fires flowed in as wickedly as the chlorine gas I used to launch upon the Boche. It was thicker than anything that ever came in from the sea at Weston, and flowed into the rooms where it hung in wreaths down the long galleries and haloed the lights with a golden haze.

I went to the Egyptian Gallery as everyone does, but felt more for the stone pieces than for the sad, rotting mummies. There were monstrous statues of Rameses II, that in themselves were just broken portions of the originals. I didn't get much from them, but there was one small, man-sized quartzite statue of Khamuas, a son of Rameses II, that thrummed with power.

I touched his bare, cool, surprisingly long feet. Why were they so long?

I know you I told it in a whisper.

That's what they all say! it replied, wickedly.

Had *I* crafted this in a previous life? Or was it the quartz speaking to me? It seemed to me that the sculptor deliberately left the heart area rough and unworked, as if this High Priest of Ptah from Memphis wanted to send us all a message:

We are not perfect; we have rough places within us that we cannot hide.

Khamuas did not need any kind of veil.

Did I?

I nodded, and moved along within my own rough body and imperfect soul.

I had hoped to see Dr. Dee's 'Scrying Mirror' in one of the other departments. It was not actually made of reflecting glass but of very smooth, black obsidian, from the Aztecs. This is a good, useful, igneous rock created when exploding lava cools. Who knows what I might have glimpsed in such a thing! I bet I could have tracked down Vivien that way, too. Or kept an eye on Fleur. And Ethel.

But it was getting darker and foggier and a hand-bell was ringing to announce closure in half an hour. I decided to leave and return tomorrow.

As I ambled through another wing toward the exit I was startled by a good humoured, slightly cynical face staring at me through the gloom. It had a curious expression, as if the owner was about to speak to me. I suddenly realised the face was larger than human, and high above my head. Then I saw the shadow of a vast wing stretching away into the gloom; a vast hoof upon a plinth. I seemed to hear Carstairs in teacherly mode telling me that this was one of the winged human-headed bulls that guarded the temples of Nineveh.

The oddest thing was, I didn't Time Travel in memory back to the hot sands of Nineveh but to the green hills around Brent Knoll, of all unlikely places. My very first glimpse of a Winged Bull was carved on the end of a bench in St. Michael's Church. It was Carstairs himself who pointed it out when the Abaris kids were invited to some festival there, and the Vicar shepherded our school to the rear away from the 'normal' worshippers.

I pulled back a bit to take in this huge and unexpected version from Mesopotamia carved from alabaster. It struck me yet again how *all* Mysteries are layered upon each other like Earth and its strata. Atlantis, Egypt, Greece, Hibernia…they are places that lie at the bottom of our mind and beneath our feet. Perhaps that's why Khamuas' feet were so long: by standing still, he was able to travel far.

Besides, which are more potent: ancient carvings from exotic realms, or modest pieces from a local English church? The person who carved that winged bull in Brent Knoll in deepest Somerset worked the same energies as the sculptor from Babylon 3000 miles and 3000 years ago. At that moment, in the British Museum near closing, Time had no more solidity than the London fog, floating everywhere, filling every breath.

It was getting darker and the hand-bell more insistent. I was about to leave when another fellow approached, oblivious of my presence in that fog-hazy room. He stood straight in a way that told of years in the British Army, as did the very worn and battered great-coat so similar to mine. He had the air of a lost and purposeless, unshaven subaltern who had been let down badly by Mater and Pater, not to mention King and Country.

I think he was having the same interplay with this Winged Bull that I had with the High Priest of Ptah. I stood further back, and further still, silently, secretly, and left him to his own devotions and his own mission. These sorts of Mysteries play themselves out all the time with **everyone**, everywhere, in 'Holy Cities' or corner-end shops. I had no need to pry.

A few moments later, lost within the fog that now blanketed the Forecourt, I only found my directions when the famous Museum Cat known simply as Mike, rubbed against my leg and purred. This was a very real beastie who had guarded the main gate since 1909, driving off rats, dogs and other interlopers. It was said that while the fierce guard-dogs of the night-watchmen refused to enter the Egyptian Rooms, Mike the Cat curled up there quite happily. Some would say it was a manifestation of Sekhmet, who had many statues in the building, or even the fiery Archangel Michael. But for me he was just a friendly furry beast who helped me direct myself[25]. Once I was onto Great

---

[25] (1908 - 1929) This was a **cat** who guarded the gates of the **British Museum. Its** fame was such that *Time* magazine devoted two articles to him on his death.

Russell Street I would make my way along to the Museum Station by touching the wrought-iron railings and hear them storying to me through the cool, damp metal. As I paused in the very centre of the gate I heard from behind me the rather desperate tones of:

Evoe, Iacchus! Io Pan, Pan! Io Pan!

And then from another direction a quite different voice giving the echo:

Io Pan!

Followed by the quite normal tones of the same echo asking:

But who is this that invokes the Great God Pan?

I had no idea what the Latin meant – if it was Latin - why do people shout when they invoke? Are the Inner Beings deaf? It is never outer volume that makes the connection, but inner intensity. Whispers are just as effective. Or am I being pompous? I can't say this is an Age Thing, because I've always been this way. Vivien often called me a 'stuffed shirt' (Do people still say that?), all because I would not take part in her own misdeeds at school.

Neither seemed aware of my presence at the gate, within the densest fog I had ever known. I should have left them to it, but I had a very human curiosity. Vivien once said that I was a 'nosy little bitch', to which I could only answer: *I am that I am* and disappear onto the hill and take refuge among the Misty People. I must admit it was quite odd and somewhat thrilling to be standing unseen within a dozen feet of two men who were exploring their own Mysteries.

The conversation between them, in the smog, had that dream-like tone I've mentioned. For a moment I wondered if this was happening on *inner* levels. Had they accidentally evoked me as a Mesopotamian priest of the Earth God?! Stranger things have happened.

I found myself listening to every word, every worry, every confession of their lives gone wrong. They had apparently had known each other in different circumstances years before, in the Army. The younger man, a former Lieutenant, expressed astonishment at this meeting. The older man, a Colonel, put their encounter down to the powers of the Winged Bull and also felt that the Great God Pan was present.

Did he mean me?

I listened. I actually thought that the younger man, down on his luck and loveless, was being groomed by his former Colonel. That happened a lot in the Army. I think the younger man was suffering from all sorts of wounds on many levels, that the older man assured him he could heal. And somehow this was all connected with that Winged Bull in the Museum.

Should I appear to them from the cloud of unknowing in which I was concealed?

*Leave be...*said Edred Son of Night, from the Darkness at the back of my mind. *This is not **your** Working[26]*.

So I let it be.

Dr. Malcolm did say that I could visit him at the Charing Cross Hospital if ever I was near there. However nice he had been to me and Fleur, offers like this from the 'higher classes' were meaningless; little better than a *Please go away now*. My French wife, Astrid, could never penetrate the miasma of words that she heard from the various Tommies she met in France, and then later among the English in England. She would often get 'betwaddled', as they said in 'Zummerzet', by what they said and what they *really* meant.

If Vivien had now moved to London, she would *have* to be near water. There were any number of parks near the hospital that held lakes: Hyde Park, Battersea Park or even St James' Park. But I felt it would need more than that, and it must involve the Moon and its tides.

In fact, I knew that the River Thames was tidal from Southend to the east of London as far as Teddington Lock some 90 miles inland. A young lad in my platoon had been a lock-keeper there before the War and he told me, wistfully, how you could dip a finger in the river and still taste salt at high tide. Vivien would *have* to be near this river. She would feel the tides and their power as you or I could feel breezes on our faces.

So I spent the first two evenings strolling back and forth along the Embankment, with the plane trees on one side and the darkly glittering hurrying water on the other. The river police chugged along downstream searching for all sorts of villains other than myself, while the evening star, great Venus, low in the western sky in the last of the sunset, stabbed its light into my brow like a sharpened pencil.

---

[26] See Ted Murchison's autobiography 'The Winged Bull' for his story.

Again, I thought of Carstairs. He was quite obsessive about Venus. He told us, jabbing his finger toward our faces, that life on Earth *actually* came from Venus; that it had been brought by a Master who brought gifts of Wheat, Honey and Asbestos, for which the primitive pre-humans were deeply grateful.

It made no sense to me, but I always loved the idea of life beyond the sky and on other planets. In the mud of the trenches we all used to thrill at the sight of the Royal Flying Corps doing battle in the skies above us. Surely it was only a matter of time before some kind of machine would reach other worlds. No doubt the visions that Mrs. Besant and Leadbeater had had about the monkey-like creatures on the jungles of the Moon will soon have their own unveiling. No doubt also there will be a layer of Mysteries one day that will be of the Stars.

Perhaps it was the energies of Venus that prodded me but I found Dr. Malcolm's rooms easily enough. He was right there in the thin London directory: 'Rupert Malcolm F.R.S.' that showed he had the top rooms in a monstrously high building in Grosvenor Road, whose concierge was a certain Mrs Humphreys.

I made a discreet visit, passing by the entrance, and was surprised to see a very young and very pregnant woman with a small suitcase pulling at the doorbell with some rage. The door opened partially and the landlady, as I imagine, hissed at this girl three times to **Go Away!** before she called the police.

But But But was all the girl could manage before the huge door was slammed in her face. Londoners could take bombing by the Zeppelins and the slaughter of her menfolk with ease, but Society scandal was too much for most of them.

The girl was dissolving in tears. Her despair was as tangible as that fog I had known the previous night. I suggested we cross the road and sit on the bench overlooking the river. For some reason she trusted me. (It was often said in the Army that I had a kindly face even when I was laying down heavy fire from my guns and slaughtering the Boche.) City men in bowlers and top hats walked past us with fixed gaze, creating their own stories in their tiny minds as the girl sobbed and sobbed.

Anita by name, her story was an ancient one and could have come straight from Babylon or any Atlantean Temple:

The Good Doctor had flirted with all three of his maids. But Anita thought she really and truly meant something to him. In her words (and she paused here) she went 'all the way'. Although the act meant everything to her, *he* was deeply ashamed. Not because of the act itself but because in our country Fit for Heroes, she was too common.

He did call me a little wretch and did have me sacked!

What could I say?

He's supposed to be a gurt toff but he does go out every night followin' women. Ark at 'Ee! If only voak knew!'

If only folk did know indeed. But I was not out to damage Doctor Malcolm himself. Not after what he did for Fleur. I just wanted to find my sister. Find him and I would find her and then I could actually save *him*. In the long run, he would become far too ordinary for an 'Atlantean Sea Priestess'; he would also be robbed and cast aside.

More tears from Anita on the bench. She looked so pitiful in her thin grey raincoat, lank hair under a headscarf that tied under her chin, her small cardboard suitcase and her old shoes.

That's a Somerset accent Anita.

Yer, Ize too common. That's what he did say.[27]

I wrote an address down on a slip of paper.

Go there and tell this woman, Ethel Maxwell, **exactly** *what happened.* **Exactly.** *She will not judge you. We plan to open a sort of school for damaged children in the near future and we will give you a job. In the meantime…*

I gave this young girl a *lot* of money, folding the big notes into a discreet bundle. Money may be the root of all evil but it's a very present help in times of need. Besides, it was not mine, it was from the Heavenly Dame of Weston to use as I felt right. This felt pure. It felt right, as if things were now flowing like the great river next to us.

She was astonished. Her face shone as if the Morning Star was behind her brow.

If you catch the next train you'll be in Somerset before tea.

---

[27] See Rupert Malcolm's confessional 'Moon Magic' that reveals he was unapologetic about this shameful act.

Her mouth was open. I noticed she pressed her hands on her knees and pushed her feet hard on the ground as if to plant futures. Then she cried in in a different way (probably with salt tears), and thanked me.

What can I do for you, mister?
Nothing.
Who be you?
Just a fella.
You be an Angel. I do know that, an Angel...
Goodbye Anita, now g'woam...

By lurking around, being invisible, I even caught sight of Malcolm and Vivien walking along the Embankment. There she was in her flowing black cloak and wide black hat, like an advert for Sandeman's Port, gliding over the ground. I would recognise her gait anywhere: she seemed to ripple from the ball of her foot to the top, swinging the folds of her cape from her square-held shoulders as rhythmically as a pendulum. Malcolm was straight and tall by her side, not quite touching, slightly stooped like an old, battered rugby player avoiding a tackle.

I had to be very careful. On two occasions I was stopped by police, wondering what a rough chap like me was up to. I persuaded them that I was just cleansing my lungs after a dose of mustard-gas during the War. They were old soldiers themselves. They understood. So I kept well back. I needed no witnesses. This went on for two nights, but on the third it was me who became betwaddled, to say the least.

This was because I actually followed Dr. Malcolm one evening when he left the Charing Cross Hospital hoping that he would lead me straight to their love nest. Instead he strolled a short distance up the road to Wyndham's Theatre, where a play called *Conchita*[28] was showing, starring one 'Lilith Morgan'.

---

[28] Reviews of that 'debut with ape' can still be found on-line. Because of Lilith's unexplained disappearance, she was replaced by her understudy, the proudly bi-sexual Tallulah Bankhead. While researching this, Daniel Steele's present publisher is startled by the fact that a musical of the *same* name is coincidentally showing at this very *same* theatre now, in 2024, starring the Drag Queen Conchita

Had she had changed her name for this new scam of hers? But a play? A *play?!*

I remembered reading in Maxwell's 'Secret Journal' how his 'Vivien le Fay Morgan' had spent a lot of time in Mexico as a mistress of Diego Rivera. Some moustachioed bandit I supposed. I assumed that Vivien was just spinning him an exotic yarn, though it could very well have been true. She also told him that she had spent some time in various pantos as the Demon Queen – or was it a Witch Queen? Of course, he swallowed the stories of his 'Sea Priestess' hook, line and sinker.

Lilith Morgan. *Lilith* Morgan!

Well, well, well… I *really* had to see this, before I created something of a Last Act for her...

Malcolm got himself an expensive seat place in the front row but I got the very cheapest one for thruppence, well to the rear, almost hidden behind a column. I bought a programme, and there she was in cold black and white:

Cast: Lilith Morgan, Miles Malleson, Charles Groves, Tristan Rawson, Barbara Gott, Lyn Harding, Mary Clare.

I smiled to see that the Playwright and Director were named as Edward Knoblock[29] and Alfred Butt respectively. *I* am not being smutty. These silly pen-names had Posh Boy Humour written all over them.

There was a full house of several hundred, I'd say, almost all male and of, I suspect, a certain persuasion. I seemed to attract a lot of

---
[29] 1874-1945. That *was* his real name.

curious glances, so I was glad when the lights were dimmed. After some tinny Spanish music from the orchestra to get us warmed up and attuned, the lights dimmed, the heavy red velvet curtain rose, and then it began.

For a moment my heart sank. I thought the actress in *very* heavy make-up and a black wig was a completely different woman. However I soon recognised my sister's gait and her unmistakeable, incantatory voice. She was playing a Spanish dancer involved with a murderous American sailor who had stout thighs, fruity tones and an ambiguous manner. It was truly dreadful, but burst into life in the second act when the pet monkey (called Thoth!) that 'Lilith' carried, stole the scene by removing her wig and waving it at the audience. It is not often that I laugh out loud, but I had to bend double and keep my face hidden from the stage. Fortunately, the rest of the audience were equally amused and they applauded the toothy creature. The ape, I mean.

'Lilith', not to be outdone by the ape and realising that the whole play was utter nonsense, then did a cartwheel showing her knickers and the audience actually roared. Despite the monkey business she received a standing ovation at the end, the most tremendous I had ever heard, like drumfire on the Somme. And Dr. Malcolm was on his feet crying *Encore!* and *Bravo!,* clapping his huge cupped hands to make them sound like exploding Mills Bombs.

I was actually proud of her at that moment.

Shame, but I would still have to kill her.

After that marvellous performance with the Ape of Thoth I quickly left the theatre and made my way back to the 'Dis and Dem' lodgings. I say 'quickly' because there were undercover police in the audience. I know that because one of them used to serve with me as a Lance Bombardier, and he gave me warning: *We're searching for a lot of fairies, Sarge...*[30]

I suppose I was searching for just one fairy of my own.

I noticed as I left that there was a storm coming. Sandbags were being placed all along the Grosvenor Road in anticipation of flooding. I expect that was Vivien's doing. Not the sandbags, I mean the actual

---

[30] Lilith's understudy Tallulah Bankhead did in fact garner a loyal but discreet band of gay followers who attended every performance and cheered her every move. Especially the cartwheels.

storm. Whenever she did her 'thing' with Wilfred Maxwell on Brean Down, we seemed to have crackingly powerful squalls that came from nowhere. I suppose the inner part of her that really was a 'Sea Priestess' played no small part. I've often been accused of causing small earthquakes myself, though they never did more than rattle a few windows and shake the tea-cups in the massed ranks of the Welsh Dressers of Weston-super-Mare, and few people even noticed.

She knew that I was near. I knew that she knew. She was my twin. Twins are supposed to have telepathies. It was not that actual words that flowed from her mind to mine, but when she was doing her magic with Dr. Malcolm I felt that 'tone' again; as if it was on a breeze.

Doing her magic...

That was a big thing to her. She always did like dressing up and lighting coloured candles and performing for the school and chanting and declaiming. The Carstairs positively encouraged her. I knew that when she was 'doing her magic' with poor Dr. Malcolm she would make it seem as if she was doing him and the world a favour.

That's exactly what she did at the Fort on Brean Down with that idiot Maxwell. I shook my head at her once after they had finished a Working and he was left gasping on the couch like a stranded eel. She said – and I remember it clearly...

What I did with him in our temple when the tide was high at Full of Moon, will go into the group mind of the race to work like leaven.

So you say.

There will be freedom in the world because of what we do.

So you hope.

We have opened a tiny rift in a great barrier and powerful forces will flood through.

So you must imagine.

You're just jealous.

Perhaps I was.

Before I found her and dealt with her, I was determined to visit the British Museum again. I wouldn't have many more chances to do so. Although the rain was still coming down in torrents there was no fog, thank goodness, and the Winged Bull from Babylon was just a lump of old and cold stone that had no particular message for me as I passed.

I'm sure it felt much the same about me. Stone can sleep as well as humans. Matter can influence Mind.

The promised display of the Marble Veiled Ladies had been cancelled, to my sharp disappointment. No explanation given. I would not now see them in my lifetime. Perhaps this particular Mystery was beyond my status or worth? I tried to be humble about this but humility has never been a virtue of mine. Instead I was determined to have another look at Dr. Dee's 'Magic Mirror'.

I had no interest in the other items of his that no doubt thrummed with energies if you cared to unlock them. It was the obsidian blackness, the dark secret of that Aztec stone that drew me. The label on the glass case said that it came from some volcano in Mexico; I think it would have told me that itself, if I could have held it. It might have been brought over by Francis Drake who was a hero to us British and a Devil to the Spaniards. It was the simplest thing, yet it was labelled as the 'Devil's Looking Glass', which Dee used to summon spirits. There was no-one else around this early in the morning. Or perhaps, as often happens, unseen Powers had arranged an invisibility spell for my own personal use. That simple black piece seemed to suck me into it. My body may have been standing outside the glass case but the rest of me was in a vortex, spinning and twisting, corkscrewing down the aeons onto a green hill not far away at all, a hill that I knew and yet did not know and never *would* know. I gasped. The picture was sharp as glass, it cut me.

I might have tried to step forward into the vision, onto the hill, into and onto that realm created by my imagination, perhaps, yet which had solid existence within my inner world.

I might have done, but I was snapped back to the present by a Voice from the back of my head that made the vision disappear, and left me standing before the case, swaying slightly.

That's the Isle of Frogs, said the Voice.

I felt a tap on my shoulder, a very physical tap, and a very physical voice from the same direction.

I say old chap are you quite all right?

I turned to see a heavily built, pock-marked fellow about my age. He looked as if he might have been an athlete in his youth, a mountain climber perhaps, but had long since let himself go. I thought he might have been a mulatto, but maybe it was just the light. How had he seen what I had seen!?

*What do **you** know about the Isle of Frogs?*

He was genuinely surprised by my question. Perhaps the Voice was mine.

Never said a word, my dear fellow. Isle of Frogs, you say? That can be on all sorts of levels. That can be more important than you know. They loved their frogs in Khem.

It was also a local and affectionate name for Brent Knoll but I wasn't going to tell him that. What was it doing popping up in Dee's Mirror?

'Old chap' and 'dear fellow'. His general manner told me he'd never worn a uniform in his life. Who does he think he is?

Who do you think you are?

Hugo Astley. Staying at the Ritz.

From his once-posh but now somewhat shabby clothes, frayed at the cuffs, I thought not.

So you say. What do you want?

I believe your sister is working some rituals at the Belfry.

I had my own small earthquake then, because that shook me. He saw my expression. He smiled.

It's all over the aethyrs. She's doing some work with that Violet Firth girl. Perhaps you saw them in Dee's Mirror just now?

I said nothing.

Your sister's Workings are important. An inner version of the electrical stuff that Dago was doing from Brean Down.

Marconi.

As I said, the Dago.

Go away.

I think he tried to hypnotise me – Me! - but pulled back. He might have felt himself teetering on the edge of obsidian volcanic depths that must have seemed like an Abyss. Dare he cross that Abyss to get to me?

No.

His tone changed.

He was still slimy.

I'm on the level, my good fellow. I would like to have copies of her rituals. I will pay you.

The night watchman, ending his shift, walked past with his slavering Alsatian and looked at us curiously. I waited until the room was empty, silent except for the ticking of a very large clock on the wall above the exhibit.

Do you know what I'm going to do, Mr. Astley – if that's even your name?

He shook his head and gave a condescending smile.

Do what thou –

He didn't finish the sentence. I punched him on the nose as hard as I could – which is very hard indeed.

As I always told the lads in my Battalion, if you get into a fight don't punch the jaw like Hoot Gibson and Douglas Fairbanks always do in the Cowboy films. You'll likely break your own fingers. The nose, however, is supremely sensitive and you can hit that without hurting yourself.

That's how I got my own broken nose. I didn't get it from Stormtroops assaulting us in the trenches during their 'Michael Offensive' in 1918. It was Vivien who broke it when I was 15, one sunny evening on the Knoll after school.

In fact it was she who taught me to fight, and fight dirty.

But that's another memory best pushed back into the Abyss of my own obsidian depths...

I still had the card that Penry Evans had given me atop of Brean Down: 3 Queensborough Terrace. I hoped to catch him in and ask about this Belfry place that Hugo Ashley had mentioned. I pulled on the doorbell of the tall and narrow Victorian building and the man himself opened it, showing delight to see me.

Thank god it's you! he whispered, beckoning me inside with finger to his lips, but naughty-schoolboy face.

The instant bond that many Old Soldiers have, made us both smile. We did seem to meet up in strange places: first on Salisbury Plain, then in Somersetshire, and now at this wearied building in the heart of Llan Dian - or the Temple of Diana as Carstairs had insisted. In fact, I had the oddest feeling as I stood on the threshold, that my old teacher was behind me, waiting to follow me in. Penry must have sensed something because he looked over my shoulder, shrugged, and then:

Sssh he whispered again, sneaking me upstairs, almost tiptoe, as the stairs were not carpeted. It turned out that 'Old Loveday', who was manager of this boarding house, wasn't keen on outsiders. It wasn't my need to ask why. The place had recently been purchased and was still rough and ready, clearly in need of a good handyman. Penry's room on the uppermost floor was full of books on medical topics beyond my comprehension. He cleared a space for me on the small sofa by pushing aside weighty tomes on tuberculosis and other scourges.

Got to keep Loveday sweet, Dan. He's paying for my training at Charing Cross Hospital.

All roads seemed to lead to Charing Cross, where no less than *six* routes meet! I'd been through there often enough myself over the years but never paid much attention to the geologies underfoot that attract lost souls and unknowing pilgrims.

He's a dear fellow. Believes that 'Love Conquers All'. Deeply in love with my Violet of course, but he tolerates me.

Of course.

I aim to be the first person in my family to become a doctor and not a steel worker like my dad and his dad before him.

Penry seemed almost apologetic. He wouldn't be the first working class follow to be accused of having 'ideas above his station'. I understood *that*. After doing a bit more of the polite and turning down his offer of a cuppa, I said:

The Belfry. Vivien Morgan. Dr. Malcolm.

Penry shrugged.

The Belfry's on West Halkin Street. Not far. You can't miss it.

Who owns it?

I don't know. It used to be a Presbyterian Church. There might have been some scandal.

It wouldn't take much to upset Presbyterians. What about Violet – I was told she was working with or for Dr. Malcolm.

Who told you that?

Hugo Astley. He tried to collar me in the British Museum.

*'Hugo **Astley**?' Is that what he's calling himself? His real name is Aleister Crowley. You must have heard of **him**.*

A bit. Not much.

He's a bit of a shit. Well, a lot of a shit. But... we keep well away.

But Violet?

Vi is seeking help from Dr. Malcolm. She's been vamping him in silly little ways to see if he can cure her epilepsy. She gets terrible grand mals, but tells people that she's actually under psychic attack.

Maybe she is!

Indeed. Maybe she is...

I told him of the debt I owed Rupert Malcolm because of what he did with Fleur.

Dr. Malcolm's one of my professors. My god that boyo gets in rages, but we can't help like him. He's got a crippled wife. Huge guilt.

Guilt?

Daniel, listen, soldier to soldier – but keep this to yourself. Soldier to soldier, he just needs a good fucking. Forget all the mind stuff that your

sister Vivian seems to be inflicting on him in the Belfry.

How do you know?

I think my Violet is quite taken with your Vivien. Sees her as a role model. They seem to talk about everything. And Vi makes a living teaching 'mind stuff' of her own in Brunswick Square. She calls it 'Orthopsychics'. It's all the rage[31].

I kept quiet. What could I say?

We talked for a little while longer, mainly about the War, then I took my leave. Before I made myself invisible to sneak back out, Penry asked:

Who was that fellow who came into the house with you?

He **had** seen him!

My old teacher from Somerset, David Carstairs. He can be a tease. Hope he doesn't cause trouble.

Vi will sort him out .

We both heard a chuckle that seemed to come from the very stones of the building. Penry smiled and closed the door silently behind me...

---

[31] See 'Priestess' by Alan Richardson, for full details that are **ONLY** in the **Thoth Publications** edition – the one that pays no royalties but is packed with info lacking in the first peely-wally edition

The Belfry was easy enough to find. I couldn't really miss it. I can't imagine the original worshippers would be happy to know who had taken over their place of worship. Then again, I had no more understanding of Presbyterians than they would have had about Sea Priestesses.

As soon I saw it, it had for me the same odd 'tone' as that many-legged Lighthouse on Burnham sands. I suppose this Belfry, seemingly a thousand miles inland, was also a sort of Lighthouse. But would it attract souls like moths to the flame? Or would it warn of dangerous rocks and their currents?

I would soon find out.

It had a big, iron-studded Gothicky door with a heavy iron latch. I knew that Vivien wasn't in. Although I would never tell her in person, my sister had such a powerful aura that it often extended well beyond her body and left traces in the atmospheres. Or maybe it was just my own atmospheres and the 'telepathies of twins' that was responsible.

As I stood there the door creaked open, even though I hadn't knocked. Before me stood a small aggressive fellow with bat ears, pug nose and velvet skull cap. He looked like he should have been in a past century helping Dr. Dee. Perhaps he lived in both times, as some seem to do.

I 'eard ye knockin' he lied. Perhaps my own aura was projecting through the door? *She said you wuz a-comin'. She ain't here. Come in.*

He turned sharply on his heel and went inside. I followed.

It was obvious at first glance that she had been spending an awful lot of Wilfred Maxwell's money on doing up what would have been a spartan and probably miserable church. There was a broad lobby that had oak panelling and dark, polished parquetry overlaying the original flagstones that I could sense beneath. On top of that there were several pale Persian rugs scattered at random, it seemed, along with deep divans, great chairs and poufs – enough for a Round Table of Knights to put their feet up and yarn about harts and hinds and helpless virgins after some hard Questing in the darkest forests in the Darkest of Ages.

The high walls had pointed arches with clear glass arched windows that looked out on what seemed like a French courtyard, and the morning sun poured through the leaves of the great plane tree that was out there. Some sort of aromatic incense was still smouldering in a silver brazier at one corner of the room, so she can't have been long gone. There was also a great hearth with a copper canopy, bigger than any dining table, piled with three-foot logs.

Come, said the gnome-man, mounting three steps to stand beside what I thought was the original altar. It turned out to be a very large stone tank that you could have swum in, though it was empty.

That, if anything, had a real 'Sea Priestessy' touch about it. I didn't want to imagine what she did with that.

The caretaker (as I assumed), lit an old clay pipe. I knew at once that Vivien would never have allowed smoking here. He was taking no small delight in the luxury.

She's gorn he told me after a few puffs and sucks to get it going. Then he turned it upside down because of the ghost-memories of German snipers who might glimpse his light even now. He looked up to the rising and spiralling smoke as though 'She' might have been a djinn following it upwards.

Where?

She's gorn to die.

I burst out laughing.

*So **you** say.*

*No, **she** said.*

I did not believe that for one moment.

I worried she might be topping herself. Had a lot of posh chaps in suits around recently demanding money. She spent £4,000 converting this place.

That would be Maxwell's money.

But Miss Lilith left a letter for you, and some other things. Follow me...

He did that spinning on a single heel thing again and led me to the very rear of building via several heavy doors. He unlocked the last one using a very large key, walked across to a mahogany desk and opened what would otherwise have been a concealed drawer.

*You **are** Mr. Daniel arntcha?*

I are.

Then he waved an envelope at me with a sort of *tra-lah* and left me alone to read it. As best as I remember it went something like:

> '*Dan, Danny, Daniel... I have been summoned by the Inner Chiefs to depart. My work here is done. It is time for me to withdraw from my body as Adepts do. I have brought back into this world a certain power which will aid the present tide of evolution. I will go to my special place and put my body into a coma. This will allow certain inner principles to withdraw to the Hall of Waiting. Then my Etheric vehicle will be able to disperse quickly. As a High Priestess of Atlantis my work has left a nucleus for the old Secret Temple work to continue. Goodbye my dearest brother and Twin Soul. Until our next life...*[32]

I gasped. The letter was almost too much for me: is this what drowning is like? A monstrous fight for breath? The caretaker heard my gasping, choking noises through the thick oak door and burst in.

Are you in pain, Sir? Is it yer ribs? A war wound? Anythink I can do?

I sat down on the desk chair, curling forward, breathless, my eyes wet with tears, staring at my feet as I placed them firmly on the ground.

Sir? Sir?

I waved him aside. That was an even better laugh than the one I had two days earlier, watching her debut at the Theatre, with the Ape of Thoth causing havoc. I had read in the local papers a French scientist arguing that the Universe began with a huge explosion from which everything expanded[33]. I felt something akin to that big bang now when I read that ridiculous letter. Such *nonsense!* She'd been reading too many Penny Dreadfuls if you ask me.

I am fine. Really.

Well, in that case sir, she also axed me ter give you this...

'This' stopped me laughing instantly. It was clearly one of the robes that Vivien had worn when flummoxing Maxwell: all the colours of the Mediterranean Sea. You can imagine them better than I can give the words. I suppose the material itself was some expensive and exotic silk, but it was the feel of the solid material it enwrapped that struck me. I *felt* them, in all their textures and colours as I shook the bundle gently, without unwrapping. It clunked.

---

[32] Gareth Knight gives the full letter in 'Aspects of Occultism'.

[33] Father Georges Lemaître. Widely scorned at the time.

Sounds like bones, sir.

I took his point. It was almost a proxy for my sister's corpse: a tangible symbol of what she had tried to become. I unfolded it on my lap, piece by piece, starting with the flared turquoise sleeves until I got to the 'bones' nestled into the womb area of the robe.

Meatyard was almost toe to toe, bending over to see the hoard of jewellery that had been stole from Dame Maxwell.

Cor blimey sir, they must be worth a fortune!

Not quite, not in earthly terms, but they had huge sentimental value for my erstwhile employer. Particularly the necklace of star sapphires and the silver moon-like head-pieces that Vivien felt would give her the Lunar powers that would change the World.

I wrapped them up again and thought of my next move. They were a large part of my reason for being here in London. That part of my Quest was over now, and I would return them quickly.

Meatyard must have guessed at my 'next move' almost before I did.

Miss Lilith said you would give me a job.

*Doing **what** for god's sake?!*

Caretaker. In that boardin' school you be gonna open.

I must admit that did rock me. I had not breathed a word of this to my sister. Had she read my mind? Or had she foreseen? Many times, as children, she would predict things for others, often when they had annoyed her – which was easily done. She would end her prediction with the words: *Thus will it be.* I don't know where she got that from; she was right more often than she was wrong. When the power was on her I sometimes wondered if she actually *made* these events happen by will-power. I had often done that myself, as I think I said, but there was usually a price to pay.

I could do anythink you wanted in the way of cleaning or cooking or fixing things or even laundry. I'm real handy, I am, jus' give me a chanst.

I looked at him. He looked at me. There was almost an astral soap bubble floating between us in which various rainbow futures swirled and glistened.

Do I pop it?

What's your name?

Meatyard. Isaiah Meatyard. 790603. 43rd Battalion Royal Tank Corps. I was Major Fuller's batman at Cambrai until I got shot.[34]

I had misjudged the man. Then – a trivial thing perhaps – but I noticed that his old Army boots were tied with such exactness that equal lengths of lace hung down on either side.

That would do me.

Very well then Meatyard. There are things I have to do now, but I'll soon be in touch.

I knowed you had a kind face, the moment I did open the door. Bless you sir!

Drop the 'Sir'. I was never an officer.

*Not outwardly – **Sir**.*

You'll have to leave London and move to Somersetshire.

*At the snap of your fingers. **Sir**!*

Stop calling me Sir.

Yessir.

The long, thrumming train-ride back to Weston was peaceful enough. I allowed myself little jabs of sleep between stations, rather like Maxwell's injections of heroin. Although there was still a major battle coming up, akin to one of General Haig's 'Big Pushes' before launching the Somme Offensive, I knew that part of my own mission was fulfilled. I would be
able to return the jewels to the Duchess and get cuddles from my daughter, and try to make a new life for myself with Ethel.

I think of Ethel and I hear the God-like General again:

*Sergeant Steele …**Do** you love her?*
She is kind, sir.
*Sergeant Steele …Do you **love** her?*
I have fondness, sir.

Perhaps in this Age, with all that I have seen and been, kindness and fondness are more than many couples have.

---

[34] Major-General J.F.C. Fuller 1878-1966. Protégé of Crowley and early prophet of modern armoured warfare, much admired by Patton and Guderian.

As for Vivien the 'Sea Priestess' and all her madness, well... that will be my own last battle before trying to dig myself into a normal life.

I mention 'digging', and that gives me a flash-back, because I had once been buried. I think this must have been the first time that anyone in the whole of the Royal Field or Garrison Artillery experienced German counter-battery fire. We didn't think anyone could be so clever as to study the incoming trajectories of our own shells and then calculate exactly where *our* cannons were placed, and thus return fire to *our* exact spot.

Although I received no credit, being a mere sergeant, it was I who suggested – insisted - that after our own salvoes we should immediately move our ordnance. This became standard practice throughout the Army. I also taught this to the American gunners under General Pershing when they joined us late (very late) in 1917. They saw my genius before my own generals did, who tended to resent the upheaval of men and materiel. They called it 'Shoot and Scoot', which I thought rather charming, and 'Scooter' was their nickname for me when we met.

But being buried....

I have heard that people who have almost drowned went through moments of great peace. Perhaps that was what Vivien had in mind when she tried to drown Fleur: a mercy killing. Did I find great peace when completely entombed? It was not *quite* like that for me.

Fortunately, I was showing a new team how to master one of the old 18-pounder quick-firing field guns that could launch anything you wanted – shrapnel, high explosive or smoke shells - for nearly five miles. I say 'fortunately' because this outdated cannon had an old-fashioned protective shield to give cover to the gunners from any warriors who might throw spears at them.

I have no memory of the explosion but I fancy that I actually saw the monstrous shell jabbing down like a finger from Heaven, just before my cannon. The next thing I was aware of was the darkness, the smell of the earth and the taste of its layers. Apparently, I was buried in a mound like a pregnant belly and when they found me – dug me out with entrenching tools and bare hands – I was curled up like a baby, thumb in mouth.

In fact I had been saved by that steel shield. And because my face was next to the opened breech where I had been about to load another shell, and its barrel poked out into the clear air, I could breathe, as babies in the fluids of the womb can breathe.

So the Earth held me, caressed me, and I felt what babies must feel when safe within their mothers' arms, against her breasts, the warmth and rise and fall of her breath. And...and... I sensed the Ghosts of the Land and its treasures and bones, and the gnomes and fays and Ancestors, and if Time itself could be 'dimpsey', it was then: murky, swirling, half-formed, spiralling with what-ifs and might-have-beens: stories overlapping stories.

I heard voices. I heard sharp steel of tools cutting into soft earth, I felt hands grabbing my ankles and pulling me out, breech first.

Steele, old chap! Must be your birthday!

Yessir. It must...

I got a lot of odd looks after that. I got the reputation, as some did, of being the man who rose from the dead and who could not be killed.

I suppose it was the mud that saved me. Perhaps an essence of the Sea Priestess diluting the hard Earth that would have crushed. Oddly enough, it was Vivien who had taught me, indirectly, the art of 'Shooting and Scooting'! When we were growing up together I noticed that she would, in various ways, target someone. She would then devise and execute a situation (often quite trivial) that would explode upon them – and then move to avoid the response. She was able to lie with such extreme self-belief and polished skill that even when I was party to the 'Truth', I was more inclined to believe her 'Untruth'.

My return was as pleasant as I hoped: a sequence of events that could have been sketched as Happy Families, though the details are hardly part of this story. I was not used to people being soft and loving, so the joy on Fleur and Ethel's faces was as precious to me as the star sapphires I had just returned to the Dame.

After she dismissed the butler, she merely gave a single sharp nod when I placed the bundle in her lap, in the privacy of her uppermost room. There was no *Thank you* as she removed her white gloves and revealed scabrous hands. My duties had been carried out as surely as the commands she gave to her butler. Did I expect gratitude from such as her? Never. When I pulled the lanyard of a cannon, knowing the cause-and-effect that would fire the shell, I had no need to *thank* the mechanism. This was her Way, the way of *her* Realm. The sun came through the uppermost windows and created a halo on her white hair as though on cue. She tapped her feet, almost like clapping. When she did speak it was brief.

*And the **Other**?*

She emphasised that last word.

Vivien was, of course, 'The Other'.

Soon, ma'am.

That was all I said. It was enough.

She nodded again then flicked her hand, as though dismissing a fly. I took it as a command to go so I about-turned, Army fashion, stamping my boots on the polished floor and went. I heard the jewellery in the bag rattling like bones as she opened it. I think I felt a sigh on the air behind me as I walked out the door. Star Sapphires can have that effect. As can precious memories.

Downstairs, in the rooms that served as an office, Scottie pulled me aside. There was something of a Yorkshire Terrier about him and he was desperate to know where I had been. I put a single finger to my lips and then his and he stopped agitating. I think he feared that one day I might pry into what he *really* did in the witch-haunted forests of the Welsh Borders before he became a 'Scottie'. His own secrets were as precious as the jewels I had just returned to the Dame. I wasn't about to rattle them.

I then learned from Ethel that the Dame had not fully washed her leprous hands of Wilfred, her useless son. In fact, she had had him committed to the Asylum at Glenside Asylum[35], where he would receive treatment for his multiple addictions and perhaps, one day, re-enter the world. After which I will predict (without using Miss Morgan's crystal ball) that he will be like the tide, affected by the Moon, coming in and out, doing the same thing over and over again.

---

[35] Glenside Asylum 1861-1994

There were secret, difficult things I needed to prepare with respect to my 'Other'. Meanwhile, almost as though I'd created another card for our Happy Families deck, Ethel had already organised a place to live for Alice. I had almost forgotten *her*! In fact, after I had given her that money on the doorstep of Dr. Malcolm's place in London, I was prepared for her to disappear and spend it on an abortion. In fact, she only took out the money for her train fare to Weston and gave the rest back to a puzzled Ethel, who was now her employer. And whose comment to me was:

She's not the brightest of souls, but she's honest and hard-working.

What could be more noble than that? So we kept her of course, pregnant or not. After the loss of life in the War, Somerset would need all the children it could get.

In fact, Ethel was happy organising this school we had planned. She did it as easily as she had ever tamed the galloping hordes of The Friendly Girls. It seems there was some old house at the bottom of their vast orchard that would serve until we could get our 'special' school up and running. Meatyard had not arrived yet, but I had no doubt that he would, and he could take on my role of odd-job man for the Maxwells.

Scottie's eyebrows rose a distance up his brow when we outlined our plans, but on the basis of 'Ask no questions and you'll be told no lies' (as our Regimental Quartermaster used to wink and whisper when he was 'relocating' supplies), he knew *just* the place for such a school as we had planned.

It's been empty for years. No-one will touch it. Supposed to be haunted – hoh hoh!

I had a sense of cruel inevitability. I told him:
It was called The Abaris. In Brent Knoll.
He frowned. He seemed puzzled. He shook his head.
Ach no! This is in Kewstoke, just up the road. It used to be a laundry.
One of those Magdalen Laundries? [36]
Aye, sort of. It closed some time ago.
I can't really explain why, but by being wrong, I felt that I had just dodged another sort of bullet.
We can walk there now if you want.

I needed the walk. Needed to feel the earth and its stratas and thus all the stratas that lie within me from the present level at Anno Domini 1922 down to the levels before the dinosaurs when the world was a molten burning glob.

Scottie gave me all the local gossip, especially about Muckley the Butcher's step-daughter Molly Coke, for whom he had high hopes. I needed no scrying mirror to be able to tell him that his courtship would stand no chance. This was not clairvoyance, but an artilleryman's logic: an analysis of energies, trajectories, atmospheric pressures and the bits and pieces of human ordnance. While he could offer her the 'corn, garth and hearth' he imagined a working class girl would want, he was in his thirties and too old. I don't mock him because there was a brief moment when I fancied her myself, despite an even greater age difference, as she seemed to like my friendly face and was a very pretty lass. But she always shied away from Fleur as though she might be contagious, or worse still, an embarrassment.

I said nothing to Scottie.

My mind wasn't fully on the building he showed me. It was off the Monks Steps, cutting through the prehistoric woodland of Worlebury Hill that I had always avoided when young.

That realm was full of the oldest ghosts – if ghosts can indeed be aged. There was a piece in the local paper last year[37] about the pits that archaeologists were uncovering. They were excited because the

---

[36] At one point there were more than 300 Magdalen Institutions for unmarried mothers in England and 41 in Ireland. The last of them closed in Ireland in 1996.

[37] The Western Daily Echo, 20/11/1921

skeletons in them showed signs of 'ritual slaying'. Excited... I'll bet none of them had served on the Front and seen the inexcusable ritual slaughter of a whole generation. Just remembering that, I had a flash memory of the entries in Maxwell's 'Journal' where he described the arrival of a Sea Priestess from Atlantis, come to organise 'ritual slayings' to control the tides.

I was part of that. Or a former version of me. The world was different then. Earth and its Time was different. We all *thought* differently about Life and its Deaths. Perhaps when I am old in this life I might be able to forgive the Germans for the atrocities they committed on their tidal wave across the flat levels of tiny Belgium. But I still won't forgive Vivien for her attempt to 'ritually slay' Fleur.

The building was directly behind old Mr. Chichester's place, where I had done good work with the walls, and almost in the shadow of the Priory that had a reliquary containing the blood of Thomas Becket. I saw a lot of phantom monks around there, as you might expect. They were not a happy lot. Still, I would deal with those echoes in due course if we took the place. The Worlebury ones from the uttermost darkness of the unreachable depths, I will leave well alone.

Scottie was in full estate agent mode extolling all the virtues of the large Georgian building made in local Bath Stone with Welsh slate tiling on its many roofs and its westward facing aspect with sea views. He must have been promised a good commission for any sales because he rattled on about the sea-gates at Kewstoke having been *fully* restored, the local rhynes cleared, assuring me that the floods in the last century would never get near the place. It was still burned into the folk memory (or is it the blood?) of when the sea-gates failed and the whole of the Vale of Avalon flooded to the depth of twelve feet as far as Glastonbury. And not long after that, in living memory here in Kewstoke, when the sea kept breaking across the land to show its power over the puny people.

I dare say, given all that, it was only natural for people to daydream about Sea Priestesses who might able to save them, as the monks in Woodspring Priory hoped that Becket's Blood would do similar, or even the simple folk of Brent Knoll building a church so that the angel Michael with his fiery Sword - or was it a Spear? – would come and save them.

He almost babbled, and lost his Scottish accent in the excitement. Not long ago he had been on a level above me as my employer. And now, thanks to erupting magma in my life, he was looking up to me.

The place was bright, glistening, and had the name THEIA[38] carved on a lintel, whatever that meant. I was surprised that I had never known of it before. That evening I asked Ethel about the place and the name. She took an old, much-thumbed book from a low shelf and flicked through it.

This is much more use than that one on Psychology. It's all about the Gods of Greece and Rome.

And Goddesses?

Especially *goddesses, Daniel. Theia was a Titaness of sight. She presides over the bright blue sky.*

I like the thought of that.

She was also the goddess that gave humanity gold, silver, and every kind of sparkling or bright gem.

Star Sapphires?

She said softly, taking my hand:

Them especially, Daniel.

There was warmth and things happening between us, on deep levels, but I did no more than return the pressure and smile.

That aside, these Titans didn't seem anything like the Giants I encountered within Brent Knoll, but I said nothing. In fact I wondered if Carstairs had fed the very word into my mind like planting a slow-growing seed into rich soil.

She was the mother of Eos the dawn, Helios the Sun, and Selene the Moon.

Did you know the Magdalen Laundry? The unmarried mothers?

I didn't. It was all very hush-hush. People kept to themselves and the women were rarely seen.

---

[38] Theia is the Greek Goddess of Sight and Visions. She was a Titan.

I want you to look it over tomorrow, Ethel, and see if it could become our special school.
I won't be secretive or discreet.
I'd be annoyed if you were.
Will you come with me – with us – me and Fleur?
I've got unfinished business in the morning...

I saw Mr. Chichester standing in his garden almost next door, looking at me like the Ancient Mariner with his long grey beard and glittering eye, ready to stop us if we got too near. I wondered if the walls I'd built him, using stones from a Christian ruin, were his attempt to keep safe from encroaching tides of an older and different sort. For a brief second, as though someone had flashed light at him using a mirror, I 'saw' him limned in fire. Had I misjudged him? Was he some kind of Fire Priest or Sun Priest from some forgotten Mystery?

I might have spoken to him but Scottie hurried us along. Although he took me inside and showed me around the many rooms, extolling the virtues of them all, the whole house was in something of a haze: Dimpsey, I might even say. I would leave it up to Ethel to make any decisions as to property. After all, her family owned half the large houses in Weston and had created a sort of White Elephant Graveyard here where, because of the War, once thriving Mansions no longer filled with the promised generations[39].

But the part of me that was Dimpseyed was already functioning on a different level. I was, I admit, somewhat 'betwaddled' as the locals would say. A small, thin layer of me, sliced like ham, was back in the British Museum staring into - sinking into - Dee's Mirror. Although the words of Scottie's spiel was going into my ears and creating pictures, there was a deeper side of me back in the Museum seeing the Isle of Frogs in that ksot unlikely of places. Not so much *seeing* it, as *being* it.

Even that is not quite what I mean.

Can a person be in two places at the same Time?
I must say **Yes** to that.
Can a person do it at Will?
I must admit that *I* cannot.
And (dear god above, below and within), can a person be Human and also Other?

---
[39] Total casualties came to 3,190,235, of which 885,138 were fatalities.

I have to think They can.

I was back within the vision that Wilfred Maxwell described exactly and accurately in his Journal, and I was under the Hill with the newly arrived but eternally-familiar Sea Priestess, as he called her. I was glared at by all those grim, skinny, shaven-headed priests who followed her everywhere and attended every whim. Eunuchs, I'd wager, though I never heard any speak. Perhaps she'd cut out their tongues. And she gave quick glances toward Maxwell-as-Was with cold indifference but more lingering and even familiar ones toward me, as though I might be her next meal. Or, as I knew at the back of my mind, her brother. And I saw them bring in the great bowl of orichalcum that was wrought with dragons and rimmed with emeralds.

And at the same Time – which is also No-Time – I was back at the boarding school in my early teens with my sister perched on the bed in the small room she had, whispering anxious things I could not quite understand. *Listen to me Danny! Listen! I'm **trying** to tell you...* but the great bell interrupted us, the bronze-age chimes rippling through and destroying the moment, and I went to supper while she huffed in her room and did without.

And I was also on the Knoll itself, and also Bell Knowle – the same place but at different levels of the same reality, and I saw the swans leaving and I heard Edred whispering and felt the Giants stirring underfoot while the underground rivers of blood and tears and overlapping Times carried all before them, hissing into unknown burning depths.

And I was back again, like the after-humming of the Abaris bell, and I was mating with the woman that Maxwell saw as a Sea Priestess from Atlantis.

You can see that I had no need to track Vivien down after the phoney 'death letter' that she had left for me in the Belfry. With 'Hugo Astley' breathing malignity down my neck, I saw in Dr. Dee's Scrying Mirror ***exactly*** where she was, and would be, and knew that in my beginning would be my end.

That's why I punched Astley so hard.

I was scared.

I don't know whether I approached the worldliness of Brent Knoll or its inner aspect of 'Bell Knowle' that morning or the next.

But the day felt 'thin'. The sky was uncannily blue. It was so blue that it was almost a Being in itself and so must be thought of as 'The Blue'. I've sometimes thought that if God could be seen as anything it would be as infinitely-aware Blueness. That makes no real sense, even to me. On the other hand, I had another small 'mind-quake' and I slid into an underlying strata of recent life events: I remembered the 11th hour of the 11th month in 1918 when the Armistice was declared and the cannons stopped and my job was done and the Silence was alive and... Insane. The sky then, where I was, was just like this – blue, blue and deeper blue that seemed to be a personal gift. So maybe some transparent, pure aspect of 'God' was involved after all. Or was this Theia, goddess of the bright blue sky who gives people jewels, making herself known to me at the last?

That still makes no sense.

And 'Bell Knowle'...

Have you ever had moments when you walked through a village, or even the street in a usually busy town, and it seemed not quite *there*? Yes, yes, the pub, the houses, the church at the foot of the hill, the horse troughs, three little shops, the blacksmith and the farrier and the red post boxes – they were all there, yet there were no signs of life, no sense of humanity. Silence as a living entity, watching me. It was as though the whole place had been constructed beneath The Blue for my benefit, creating a world that was neither here nor there, existing in some hidden place between the almost-touching realms.

I stood at the rusting iron gates of the Abaris school and looked through the bars at what remained of the building, now collapsed within the enclosure of its high walls. The area was smaller than I remembered. You might have said a bomb had dropped, but none of the Zeppelins had got this far West, and not even the biggest of Big Berthas had this range. Unless you knew, it was hard to imagine that there had been anything of substance here at all. The Carstairs had seemingly upped to London and disappeared from the world entirely, taking their own realms with them.

In fact, after that disastrous fire, the school had been scavenged by the locals during the War. Every useful piece of stone, or iron or wood or glass or crockery was taken for their own needs during those austere and dreadful times when German submarines caused havoc to our supplies.

As I looked through the bars I re-assembled the broken walls on their cracked foundations and levelled the floors as though I were some super-Mason and Master Carpenter. I put layer upon layer of memory, levelling everything in sequence until I could see the pointed roof and the smoking chimneys. In an instant my whole Past was there, intact if a bit wobbly.

I was never wobbly during the War, when this sort of destruction was an everyday reality. I don't remember ever being liked at school, but I became popular among the Tommies and our young subalterns, especially, whose life expectancy at the Front was reckoned to be 7 weeks. It was not because of my personality (which was once described as being cold like granite, underneath the 'kind face'), but because I had a sense of when to take cover. This was nothing to do with keeping below the parapet to avoid snipers, but because I usually knew when Fritzy was about to pound us. Perhaps I had a telepathic connection to my peers, like-calling-to-like across No Mans Land.

Perhaps I just sensed that the atmospheric pressures and wind were right for launching a few salvos. Of course, I knew all the shells they ever devised and then launched. I could spend all day listing them and their effects. I was bit a like the cranky ornithologists you often meet in Somerset Levels, except I dealt in the habits of flying metals and their explosive contents, rather than exotic birds. Even their names had colourful plumage: There were the Black Marias - huge howitzer shells that sent up stinging, blinding smoke; there were the Coal Boxes which were noisier than any express train and left heavy black clouds of poisonous gas; there was the Rum Jar, the Flying Pig, the Ypres Express and worst of all was Big Bertha, a monstrous wench that fired on us from 12 miles away and sent a twelve hundred pound shell we called a Jack Johnson, named after that heavyweight black boxer from America. When that one came over the air was displaced so suddenly that anyone within range would be knocked over by the rush.

After that one time when I had been buried in the earth, I developed a keen sense of when we might have another and the lads around me seemed to notice this. Whenever I had the compulsion to move position, take up my gas mask, put on my steel Brodie helmet and grab some food and water, they quietly did the same. I think I became some kind of talisman toward their own survival. Some of the younger ones, at times of extreme fear, called me Dad.

I suppose you think I'm rambling, and I am. Trying to get a breathing space. Buying time. It's because, under the pure blue sky and its quietude, I heard a noise which made me tremble in a way that Big Bertha never did.

Breaking the glassy, sparkly lull of that infinite moment I heard the unmistakeable brass sound of the school bell that once organised my days into: Waking, Lessons, Playtimes, Meals and Lights out. It seemed to vibrate – I should actually say explode - at some point between my heart and throat. I know that shell-shock could cause huge ruptures within the brains of other men, but I was always, somehow, beyond that. Yet that bell, with its single rhythmic chimes, took me back into another strata of awareness of a time before the War, before the Army, before my adoption by the Carstairs, before the darkness of my origins – a sound that made *me*, iron-hard Sergeant Daniel Steel of the Royal Field Artillery, shiver...

I had to follow it...

The heart shaped top of the hill was smaller than I remembered. Yet it was an entire world. I had no sense of the countryside around, no hint that it was even in the world. From this summit, as a boy, I had once communed with Giants, Fays, fierce Elementals and sensed the ebb and flow of great battles in times gone past. Now, beneath the dome of the Blue, there was just, at the very tip of the heart, my sister Vivien. Ringing that damned bell. She was barefoot, wore a flowing blue dress and had no make-up for once. I noticed that her loosened, shoulder-length hair was streaked with grey. She looked old. I heard her voice in my mind:

'So do you!'

She kept ringing, great swings of her right arm, but slower this time.

Here at last, Dan Danny, Daniel. I don't want to fight you.

I shrugged. I knew of old that if I traded words she could twist me like a piece of Celtic knotwork.

Besides, if I had wanted to fight you I would have chosen the sea shore.

I shook my head.

My sea will always be more powerful.

I shook my head again, thinking of the Earth with its crust of solid rocks and minerals, above the mantle and burning core. All vaster and older than the Sea of which she was some sort of Priestess.

'Some sort of priestess', did you just think at me?

She was good, I'd give her that.

Those days are gone, Vivien. You are as false as that bell. It looks like the one we had at Abaris but it's not the same. An inferior metal, probably from Mexico.

Yet it works. Isn't that the important thing?

Isn't it important that you ruined Wilfred Maxwell.

I transformed him. You should have seen him before. Twerp.

I didn't know the word, but her tone explained it.

He's in the asylum

He'll come out. He will steal his miserable mater's jewels again and marry that empty little Molly Coke.

I thought of poor Scottie and the hopes he had.

Don't frown Danny. It spoils your kind face. Wilfy boy won't be able to get it up with Molly unless she pretends to be me. It won't end well. Thus will it be...

Silence. Between us. Around us. Above and Within us.

You don't remember do you, Dan, Danny, Danieeeeel?

The school? The Carstairs?
Carstairs wasn't fully human, you know.
I supposed not. There were a lot of such people around.
*Nor are **we**, Viv.*
Well, what we are no-one can ever know.
And they will never find out.
Actually, I thought Carstairs was a bit of a phoney. A bit.
And his wife?
She frowned.
*Don't remember **her**.*
Aren't we all phoney? And hiding. We're all acting, in some way.
We both had the same quick memory, of that night in the Wyndham Theatre with the Ape. We both laughed.

*I **knew** you were there! You actually spooked the monkey. I could have started a new career but for you.*
Apologies.
Accepted.
It was a nice moment, but I still had to kill her.
For an instant I had a to-and-fro from that splinter of my conscience that I call 'General Haig'. I stood to attention inwardly, which meant I had to be straight and clean, utterly correct and honest:

*Sergeant Steele …**Did** you love her?*
She is my sister.
*Sergeant Steele … Did you **love** her?*
She is my twin.
*Sergeant Steele!! ATTEN-**SHUN**! Did. You. Love. **Her**?*
With all my heart, on this heart-shaped hill.

She rang the bell once more. If notes from a brass bowl being struck by an iron clapper could express sorrow, they did.
You still don't remember what happened here, or why I'm ringing this stupid bell that you used to love so much.
I was suddenly back within the vision described so clearly in Maxwell's 'Secret Journal' that everyone in Weston-super-Mare knew about by now: The Sea Priestess coming to us for a sacred mating from what *he* thought was Atlantis, but was really Barry Island in Wales. The dreadful, hairless eunuchs she brought with her as body guards; and me

as the hairy, horny King of the Hill was who was also her brother, and with whom she must mate.

That's what your 'Sir Edred son of Night' is. I suppose he must our great great great great great thousand-times-great grandson.

I'd never thought of that.

*No, no, you 'never thought of that'! But that's NOT what I mean! Remember the last time we spoke in school? The **very** last time? Before I 'disappeared'?*

She rang the bell madly again, I thought her arm might drop off. If the rest of the world below or around the hill existed it would have woken everyone.

*I sat on the edge of the bed trying to tell you something. Something that was actually important. Something utterly and **completely** important. I begged and pleaded for you to listen but when you heard the stupid bell you had to go running off to supper.*

I was afraid. I didn't want to hear. I tried to deflect:

You wanted to sacrifice Fleur.

NO I DID NOT! Stop trying to deflect. You sound like Maxwell.

I tried to find deep places for my mind to hide, in the Earth beneath my feet, but there was nothing. No 'caverns measureless to man', no million-year strata, no rivers of fire and blood that might sweep me away. Nothing.

Actually, Dan, Danny Daniel, this is where it happened. This very spot. This is where our lives changed.

What could I ask? What dare I ask? There was no sort of lanyard in my life at that exact moment that I could pull and send an offensive salvo over the far horizon. The enemy was here. They were my sister.

*What. Did. I. **Try**. To. Tell. You?*

I shook my head. A pathetic shake. I shrugged a pitiful shrug.

I needed to tell you, ached to tell you, cried all day and about it.

Honestly, beneath The Blue dome of this sacred hill, under the gimlet eye of 'Haig', my mind was as blank and black as an obsidian mirror. I could only ask:

What!?What?!

That I was Preg and Nant. Pregnant.

I went silent. This was beyond my imagination. I had to ask, weakly and with complete ignorance, using the first name that sprang to mind:

But who? Carstairs?

She did not shout, though she could have done. She did not snarl, though it would have been acceptable. Her words hissed like a missile from a trench mortar.

You. You idiot. Imbecile. Moron. Lunatic and long-lost brother of mine. Or maybe you've got an inner Mongol stopping you from understanding?

A modest shell falling close to a man might not explode but it will cause concussion, or nerve shock. Something seems to break in the brain. If a man is very near a large shell, he will not only be knocked to the ground, but crushed to pulp by the same tremendous force that shatters buildings to rubble and dust. A man can be lifted high in the air out of a trench by the concussion of a shell.

None of those could compare with what I felt then. I could not find words. I twitched. The breath in my throat croaked. I was a frog on the Isle of Frogs.

You've chosen to forget, Danny. But it was here, at the point of this heart. It was a lovely day, sunny, all fire and air. I curved above you and cast a shadow on your kind but stupid face. You pretended to resist. I forced myself on you while the church bells rang. I wanted you to be my first. It had to happen.

I remembered – Nothing. Not here, not then. Yes, yes yes I remembered that holy mating in the Cave below the Hill when the Sea Priestess came to me from 'Atlantis'. Had that wave of memory swamped and dissolved the later events Vivien just described?

Preg. Nant. They sound like places in Wales, don't they? Pregnant. You'll remember soon. Like one of your nasty shells ripping your concrete head open.

I croaked again.

You were afraid of me. Most men are. I had to have you.

I sat down under the infinite bowl of The Blue, at the very tip of the hill's heart-shape. There was nothingness within me, nothingness to the east, north, west or south. I could not sense Below. There was nothing that any Earth Priest could grab.

Carstairs sent me away.
To the 'Theia' house? For unmarried mothers?
Yes, but only until the baby was born.
The baby...
A boy.

Some explosions can deafen, while leaving your body intact. It feels like being enclosed in a genie's bottle of clear but very thick glass. The world goes on around you, you have your own wishes sealed in with you but everything around is untouchable.

I was 13 and a bit – I think. I would have left school soon anyway. So they sent me away. I didn't get to spend any time with our baby.

'Our baby. **Our** baby' she said. That was a sniper's bullet into my forehead. I should have kept my head below the parapet – but how could I?

Was it... was he...

Normal? Yes, and beautiful.

I was at the moment of Armistice again. The War had stopped and the future had not yet begun.

Where did you go?

Llandudno. They found me a job skivvying in a grand hotel. They were nice.

Viv...

Actually... *I came back to the school to find you. Carstairs opened the door a crack but wouldn't let me in. He said: 'The young Master is over the hills and far away'.*

I ran away too, joined the Army. Did you ask his wife?

I don't remember her. He was afraid of me. A lot of men are.

All of my working life, the only real 'Word of Power' I've ever known was 'FIRE!' when I pulled the lanyard and launched another screaming Death into the skies. The only thing I could replace it with now was the very lame, very quiet:

Sorry...

We lay on the grass, facing each other, having our own truce. Her long blue dress flowed like a deep stream upon the grass. Me on my right side, her on her left, an illusion of Water and Earth between us. I seemed to remember things, tiny things, like plants pushing up through the soil. They could wait.

How would you have killed me Danny?

I'd thought of that a lot over the months.

I would have gone to a deep place, into my very core, back to a time when the Earth itself was being formed. I would have stopped the essence of the Earth Priest emerging. And, because you're my twin, that would have killed the Sea Priestess.

She laughed. Her whole body rippled. I'd forgotten what a nice voice she had, almost hypnotic, certainly seductive.

Actually, Danny that is ridiculous. You've been reading too many novels. You know you cannot kill me in any way.

I promised the Dame.

Bugger the Dame. You won't be the first. I know what went on in her upper rooms with those matelots. You owe me. You know that.

I did. I had to sigh.

Yes. I do owe you.

Silence. Stillness. A truce that passeth understanding.

I will now disappear from this narrow little world of yours. Go home and tell good lies. Say that the 'Sea Priestess' is dead. Then start a new life with your hunchy-necked woman, raise Fleur for her remaining years, start your 'special school' and then...

She paused. Turned her head to the sound of the bells in St. Michael's Church that were driving off demons in the village below. The Blue was now no more than a flecked and grey sky with scudding shoals of mackerel clouds. On the slopes around I could hear the panting of the great tethered horses pulling the heavy ploughs through the soil. I could feel the curved iron of the blades cutting through the waves of brown earth.

...And then one day I will appear as if by magic and you will help me find our lost child. We will do this secretly, so you can still live as a 'normal' man.

How could I refuse? The doors of an unknown Treasure House of Images was opening before my inner eyes. This was more valuable than any jewels or minerals I'd ever held or destroyed.

Viv, sister mine, Ethel doesn't have a hunchy-neck, your ankles are definitely getting thicker, and you do need make-up at your age. But... I will do all that. And we will find him, using all our powers of Earth and Fire, Water and Air.

You sound like me, a bit phoney.

I am you, and I make things work.

She smiled. She looked wonderful. Ye gods but I loved her.

She read my mind in that place shaped like a heart.

You always did.

The mist from the sea came in and the world was dimpsey again.

Thus will it be...

British Sign Language finger-spelling

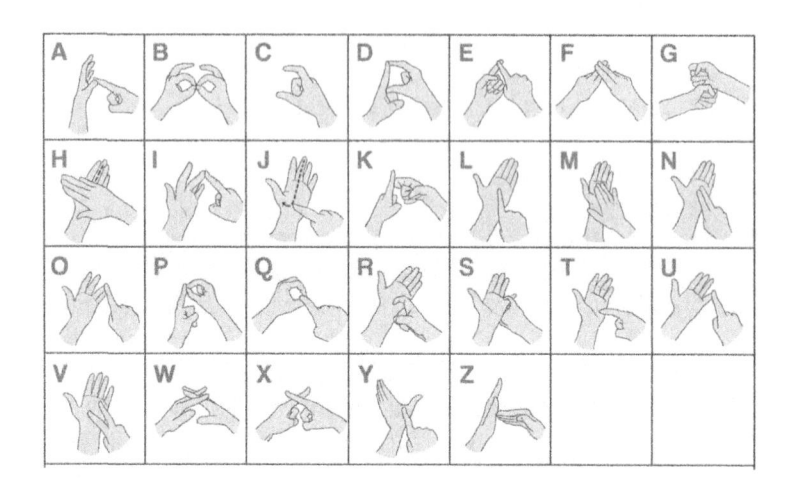

Danish, French and American Sign Language finger-spelling

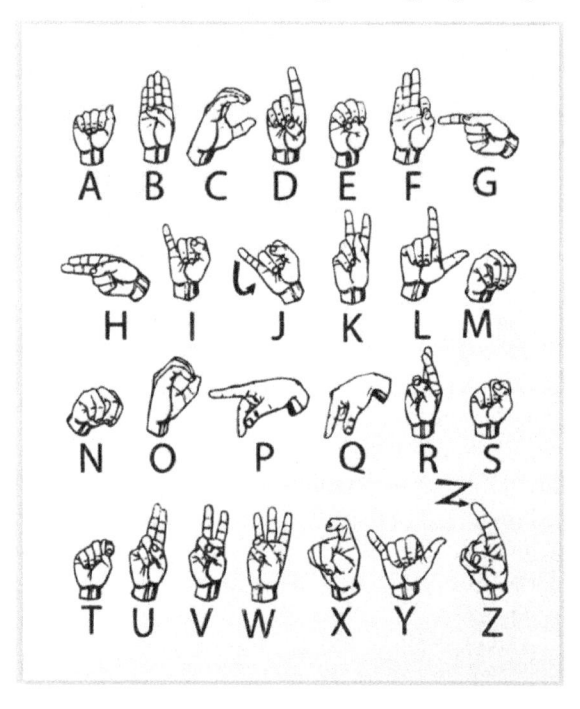

Printed in Great Britain
by Amazon